The Opening Eye

Dr. Frank McGillion, who was born in 1948, is a graduate of Glasgow University. He has carried out post-graduate studies at several universities in the U.K. and holds a Ph. D. in Clinical Pharmacology from Glasgow University. He is the author of a number of specialized papers in various branches of the biological sciences. He has studied astrology for some years and at present he lives in London and, in addition to writing, works with a major pharmaceutical company.

The Opening Eye

Frank McGillion

Coventure Ltd London

Published by Coventure Ltd.
20 Essex Street, London WC2

Photoset and produced by
R James Hall Typesetting & Book Production Services
Harpenden, Herts
Printed in Hong Kong

ISBN 0 904575 03 9

To

Marianne and Jennifer

Acknowledgements

I would like to thank the following for permission to use previously published and copyright material:

The MIT Press use of their cover design from *Frontiers of Pineal Physiology*, 1975.

Science News, the weekly news magazine of science, copyright 1976, by Science Service Inc.

Hodder & Stoughton for material from *Supernature* by Watson, L., 1973.

Chaucer Publishing Company, for material from *Human Context* by Morano, D.V., 1975.

R.K.P. Princeton University Press, for material from *Synchronicity: an acausal connecting principle* by Jung, C.G., 1972.

W.H. Freeman & Company, for excerpts from "The Quantum Mechanics of Black Holes", by Hawkins, S.W., *Scientific American,* Jan. 1977.

Macmillan Publishing Company for the diagrams of the sensory homunculus (fig. 19) from *The Cerebral Cortex of Man* by Penfield, W., and Rasmussen, T., copyright © 1950, renewed 1978.

I would also like to thank Miss M.S. Sisley, for her help in the preparation of the manuscript.

Contents

Figures and Tables

Foreword

Perhaps the most important feature of this book, and its recurrent theme, is the pineal gland.

It has not, however, been possible, nor indeed was it intended, to give a comprehensive discussion of the functions of the pineal gland in this work. Such a book will be published at a later date.

Introduction

'A lonely impulse of delight' drove me to write this book. At least, the man who first wrote that line did. Some years ago I discovered that W. B. Yeats, whom I much admire as a poet, was also an astrologer. I found it puzzling that this eminent statesman and literary figure could be attracted to a subject which I considered obvious nonsense, though I knew almost nothing about it.

When I was given a copy of a book called *Astrology and Science* I gave it considerable attention in order to understand Yeat's preoccupation. I was impressed by the content of the book. It claimed statistically significant correlations between planetary positions at the time of a person's birth and their subsequent choice of profession. Despite its title, the book effectively discounted traditional astrology as Yeats would have known it and simply presented impressive evidence that the planets seemingly affect us. As a result I read further on the subject.

It didn't take me long to understand why Yeats had been drawn to it. The symbolism, mystique and abstraction of the subject were finely balanced with the precision involved in utlizing astrological techniques. The subject was understandably attractive to the poet as its form was similar to that of his art. By training, however, I am a scientist, not a poet, and it was the statistical evidence in favour of the subject more than its mystique which, initially at least, preoccupied me.

As I progressively realized that there was scientific evidence that the planets could 'affect' us, I wanted to know *how*.

I soon came to realize that there are a number of possibilities as to how planetary positions and movements at the time of birth could influence us, but for certain reasons (some of which will become clear later in the book) I formed a rather singular idea . . . perhaps the influences of astronomical factors at the time of birth could affect the function of the pineal gland and hence the subsequent development and behaviour of the individual.

It is appropriate here for me to give an operational definition of astrology. For the purposes of this book I would define it as being 'the study of the influence that the planetary positions at the time of our birth have on our subsequent development, or the effects they have on our behaviour at any time'. This, as I have said, is an operational definition and not one which astrologers would necessarily accept.

My intention has been to demonstrate that we are capable, in acceptable scientific terms, of providing a model to account for some astrological observations as operationally defined. I have offered what I consider to be credible hypotheses, not explanations. Inevitably there are occasions when I have discussed traditional astrology. For those unversed in this I have included an appendix briefly describing its principles.

To argue a credible scientific case for even an attenuated form of astrology requires a multidisciplinary approach with all its attendant problems. Specialist readers may feel disturbed that the subtleties of some subject matter are not fully discussed, and more general readers may find themselves presented with chapters of quite different and perhaps seemingly unrelated content. In the end, however, such problems should fall into their true perspective and hopefully a cohesive picture will emerge.

I have endeavoured to make the book entertaining as well as informative and consequently have added pieces of material here and there which hopefully achieve this end.

I believe that some of the material contained in this book is of that special nature which will make some of us reflect on the nature of the universe which we inhabit. This applies as much to the acceptable wonders of contemporary physics as it does to such obscure observations as the fact that the planets 'appear to play music' as they spin around us.

London 1980

CHAPTER I

The Third Eye Reopens

In 1894 an inquisitive gentleman named Cook informed the medical profession of the singular fact that Eskimo women had a four-month cessation of menstruation during the long nights of winter which exist inside the Arctic Circle.[5] Dr. Cook also established, by means undisclosed, that there was also a decrease in sex drive in both males and females at this time. Fortunately he found that with the onset of spring, when the nights become shorter, both menstrual flow and natural instincts returned to normal and then the ice melted.

The term 'menstruation' is of course derived from the Latin *menses* meaning month, this derivation reflecting the periodic reproductive cycle in non-pregnant adult women which corresponds more or less to the monthly cycle of the moon of about twenty-nine days. In fact, to be more precise, it would appear that the duration of the menstrual cycle is not just more or less that of the monthly lunar cycle but is exactly that.

In 1959 and 1967 Abraham and Walter Menaker published papers describing correlations between lunar periods and reproductive cycles.[20][19] Using large numbers of subjects, they found that the lunar month and the average menstrual cycle were both 29.5 days in duration. Further, the period of normal gestation was found to be 265.8 days, or precisely nine lunar months. They also reported that significantly more births occurred at full Moon than at any other time of the month.

The Moon, of course, reflects sunlight onto the Earth and it is aesthetically pleasing to find that light itself can apparently synchronize the menstrual cycle. If the menstrual cycle is irregular, say twenty or thirty-six days instead of the usual twenty-eight or twenty-nine, then simply by exposing the person exhibiting this irregularity to light, normality, it is claimed, can be restored.

This rather remarkable observation was reported in 1967 by Dr. E. M. Dewan.[7] He had produced this effect in a number of women by a very simple technique well exemplified by quoting the case of his first reported subject. She was a young woman with a history of irregular menstrual cycles for sixteen years. During the fourteenth, fifteenth and sixteenth nights of her menstrual cycle (the first day of menstruation counting as day one) her bedroom was kept illuminated by a bedside lamp on the floor while she slept. After four months of this, her cycle, which had in the past ranged from twenty-three to forty-eight days, synchronized to one of twenty-nine days.

The fourteenth day of the menstrual cycle is, of course, the time when ovulation occurs in most women. The ovum passes down the Fallopian tube and embeds itself in a prepared uterus awaiting a spermatozoic suitor. If none arrives and conception does not occur, then at about the twenty-eighth day the wall of the uterus breaks up and produces menstrual flow.

If, however, conception does occur this process doesn't begin and menstruation doesn't take place. Again, it is aesthetically pleasing to note that light can also affect ovulation and thus, of course, conception.

In 1968 a study was published by Timonen and Carpen in which the authors reached the following conclusion: ovulation and super-ovulation (production of multiple ova), and consequently conception, was markedly and significantly affected by the season of the year.[27] They based this conclusion on the observation that more conceptions occurred in summer than at any other time. This effect was more marked the more extreme the latitude. In other words, the further north you went in summer the more likely you were to conceive. Furthermore, the percentage incidence of conception of twins or triplets also increased. This latter fact particularly indicates that this effect is not simply a social one due for example to increased sexual activity occurring at holiday time. It implies that what we have here is a true seasonal variation in ovulation patterns which is proportional to extremity of latitude.

These findings, obtained from a study in Finland involving over 300,000 subjects, draw a neat comparison with Dr. Cook's findings that in winter Eskimos did not menstruate and did not conceive.

The questions beg themselves: what could affect libido and ovulation in a way which could cause seasonal vagaries in conception? What is common to long winter nights, long summer days, extremes of latitude and bedside lamps kept on between days fourteen to seventeen of irregular menstrual cycles? Light—its presence, variation or absence!

In 1971, C. A. Elden, taking into account all relevant factors, predicted that in the state of Washington in that year one hundred and twenty children should be born to women who had been blind from birth.[8] One was born. For the whole of the U.S.A. in that year predicted births of children to congenitally blind women indicated that one thousand children should have been born to them. Six were born.

For many years no definite correlation could be established between any physiological factor and age of onset of menstruation. The most accurate correlation now known to us is that the degree of bone development in girls is related to age of onset. Even so, it had been known for many years that onset of menstruation in blind girls was earlier than that

3

in non-blind girls. However, Elden had apparently now established that blindness from birth could mean that a woman was effectively sterile. It need not be stressed, of course, that blind people are unresponsive to light.

It seems, therefore, that by some mechanism light can affect the reproductive process. We shall discuss soon how this could occur. At present, however, I should like to side-step a little and take a look at another phenomenon in humans which also seems to follow a definite pattern, and which again appears to be related to season of birth and hence to time of conception. This is the condition known as schizophrenia.*

For many years it has been suspected, and now it seems certainly established, that people who subsequently become mentally ill and are diagnosed 'schizophrenic' are born, and hence conceived, more frequently at specific times of the year. Torrey et al., 1977 have collected data on over fifty thousand 'schizophrenics' and concluded that there is a highly significant peak in 'schizophrenic' births (i.e. birth of people who subsequently become schizophrenic) from December through to May in the northern hemisphere, with a marked peak in March. The opposite effect is evident in the southern hemisphere where there is a marked peak in September.[28]

The evidence from this study, therefore, would suggest that there is a winter and spring seasonal peak of schizophrenic births which is maximal at about the time of the vernal, or spring, equinox—the time when day and night are of equal length.

In the case of schizophrenic births we cannot simply pre-

---

* In the context of this book the term 'schizophrenia' is used to describe patients who have been psychiatrically thus diagnosed. It is well accepted that the term is not precise and that it may be used to desscribe mental states which are quite possibly unalike. Patients termed schizophrenic, however, have common symptoms of withdrawal, delusions, hallucinations etc. Irrespective of the debate as to what is or is not schizophrenia, the fact reamins that patients who are mentally ill, and termed thus, are born more frequently at certain times of the year.

sume that because they occur most often at particular season of the year and come to a peak at the equinox, they are correlated with photoperiod (the ratio of light to dark during a 24 hr period) in the same way as ovulation and conception appear to be. Many other factors of a nutritional or environmental nature also fluctuate with the seasons, and could be responsible for predisposing an infant to subsequent mental illness. Infectious diseases, for example, demonstrate seasonal periodicity and could be contributory to such effects. It is *possible*, however, that photoperiod could be a factor in predisposing the infant to mental illness and we shall discuss this in the final chapter. In the meantime, what could be better than to take a look at eyes?

* * * * * * * * * *

When the female octopus spawns, her eggs float out and grow. They hatch and she dies, killed by a secretion which she has in some way released from glands in her eye.[31] To a dog or cat the most exquisitely coloured garden of flowers is simply a mixture of black, white and shades of grey. To a bee the flower which is pale and uninteresting to us is gleaming with waves of violet blue light. Different eyes, different worlds.

Eyes are intriguing organs—visible parts of the brain, carefully developed and refined over centuries of evolution. We rely on them greatly and accept that blindness is one of the most disastrous of human afflictions. So we do, and should, duly appreciate our eyes. All three of them.

Our eyes are very important, and this not only means the two that see themselves in the mirror every morning but the other one also, the third eye which, responsive to light just like its external counterparts, tucks itself snugly away in the shadows of the brain. (Fig. 1)

To Buddhists the third eye when opened looks into the haunts of things ineffable. To Descartes it was the 'seat of the soul', the ghost in the machine which controlled its

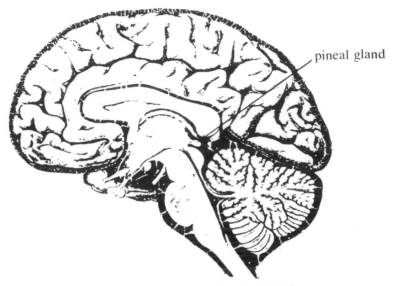

Figure 1: Position of the pineal gland

movements. To most physicians and scientists, until fairly recently, it was an anachronistic remnant of evolutionary development, a sort of appendix stuck in the middle of our heads. It is perhaps none of these things, but neither is it any brain-hidden nonentity. The pineal gland, as the third eye is now called, has metaphorically reopened, and has allowed us to observe at least part of its very significant activity.

The term 'pineal' is derived from the Latin *pinus* meaning 'pine cone'. It is a cone-shaped organ which in man weighs about 100 mg and in smaller mammals, like the rat, about 1 mg. It is situated near the centre of the brain enclosed within the two cerebral hemispheres, and is about 8 mm long.

The human pineal was apparently first described around 300 B.C. by the Greeks Herophilus and Erasistatus who attributed to the organ a 'memory valve' function. When your memory was blocked, a shake or sharp tap on the head would clear the valve and your memory would flow normally

again. A number of illustrious thinkers, including the celebrated Roman physician Galen, rejected this ingenious idea,
but it's interesting to observe that the concept of the pineal
as a valve persisted. As recently as the nineteenth century a
physician named Magendie suggested that the pineal was a
valve which regulated the movements of 'cerebral fluid',
the watery liquid which flows within our brain and spinal
cord.[18]

It was in 1640 that Descartes described the pineal as the
'seat of the soul' in a letter to a certain Father Mersenne.
Despite the persistence of this concept, due probably to the
immense success of Cartesian philosophy in general, most of
Descartes' contemporaries dismissed the idea as fanciful, and
few were sympathetic to it. Gradually the concept lost
support and other less elevated functions were attributed
to the pineal. For example, in the eighteenth century the
idea was prevalent that madness was a consequence of pineal
abnormality, and in a book published in 1786 'stony hard-
ness of the pineal gland' was listed as one of the causes of
mental illness.

By the mid-nineteenth century, however, the pineal, in
the Western world, was gradually being relegated to the realm
of the vestigial; and for a century thereafter it was considered
to have no function whatsoever. The eye had closed and gone
to sleep.

It is not uncommon for the pineal to sleep—at least according to some groups of mystical bent. The opening of the
third eye in many Eastern religions is considered to be
associated with the attainment of spiritual awareness, or at
least is a step in that direction. While the third eye sleeps the
aspirant remains unaware of the ineffable. Many techniques
are available to enable aspirants to 'open' it: these range from
systems of meditation taught in Yoga (which literally means
'opening') to crude, if somewhat apocryphal, surgical techniques which, if indeed they are practised, presumably open
more than is intended.

Take a glance at some religious work of art from the East
and you will observe a face with the mysterious eye inscrut-

ably staring out at you from the middle of the forehead like some over-endowed Cyclops. The Hindu caste mark is placed at a site which is commonly chosen to symbolize the 'eye', and in this case the colour of your eye tells a great deal about your spiritual development. In the roots of Western culture too, particularly in ancient Egyptian art, the third eye is far from inconspicuous.

To certain adherents of Yoga, Man has seven centres of vital force termed 'the Chakras' (Fig. 2). The word *chakra* means 'wheel' in Sanskrit, and these centres are considered to be wheels or vortices of energy which correspond to the assumed seven levels of Man's real and potential consciousness. The axis of the chakras is the spinal cord and all seven lie along its length. They are termed root, sacral, solar, heart, throat, brow and crown chakras. The last, which is thought to be situated at the pineal,* is considered the seat of the highest level of consciousness—the spirit. In pictures of holy people painted by discerning artists the crown chakra is depicted as being open by the presence of a halo around heads.

The pineal, therfore, has for centuries been considered as having some mystical significance, and perhaps not without reason as will become clearer later. It seems most unlikely that Rene Descartes wrote much of his prodigious work sitting in even the half-lotus position; however, he and his Eastern counterparts had at least one thing in common—they agreed on the 'seat of the soul'.

A number of people, therefore, have believed that when the third eye opens it is very illuminating. When after a few centuries it opened again in the 1950s, this proved to be the case.

In 1954 two scientists by the names of Altschule and Kitay reviewed all the available literature on the pineal

---

*To many esotericists the pineal corresponds with the brow chakra. For reasons which will not be discussed here I have taken it to be the physical correlate of the crown chakra. Anyone interested in the esoteric explanation of the role of the pineal in this context is referred to specialist works, e.g. *The Secret Doctrine* by H. Blavatsky.

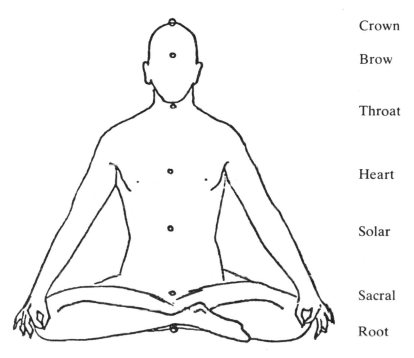

Crown

Brow

Throat

Heart

Solar

Sacral

Root

Figure 2: The Chakras

gland which had been produced by the scientific establishment.[16] They concluded that while most studies on the gland had produced inconclusive or negative results, a few studies indicated that the pineal was active and had some biological role. The nature of this role, however, was by no means clear.

The normal way to study how a gland functions is to remove it from the body and see what happens. For example, Banting and Best removed the pancreas from a dog and found that the animal died of diabetes. When in 1922 they did the same with another dog, but gave it injections of extracts from the pancreas, it survived. These extracts, of course, contained insulin which is produced in the pancreas, and, as a result of these studies, the function of insulin and the

9

'cure' for diabetes was discovered. Such a relatively simple approach cannot be carried out with the pineal, which is one of the reasons it took so long to discover its functions.

To begin with, in the early stages of pineal research when techniques for its investigation were developing, it was difficult to remove the pineal from the animal without killing it, and a dead animal doesn't tell us much about the effects of hormone deficiency. However, other major factors were responsible for the delay in discovering pineal function. These were unrecognized at first and almost totally unsuspected.

Unlike most other glands, the pineal's function changes with the age of the animal, with the day/night cycle, and with the degree of environmental illumination in general. Its function also changes with the seasons. This meant that, because people researching on the gland worked on it at different times, places and seasons, a host of discrepant results about its functions appeared. One study would clearly demonstrate, for example, that it suppressed sexual activity in rats; but when researchers in another country repeated what was ostensibly the same study at a different time, the pineal seemed to make rats quite the opposite. It was only when these seasonal and circadian (daily) changes were recognized in the 1960s that the mysterious eye stopped winking with amusement and began to release its secrets.

The source of the answer to most of these secrets was the discovery in 1958, by Lerner and others, that the pineal produced and released a hormone, hitherto unknown, called 'melatonin'.[17]

The pineal manufactures melatonin by a series of relatively complex reactions (Fig. 3). Firstly the amino-acid tryptophan, which we obtain from our food, is converted into a substance called 5-hydroxytryptophan by an enzyme called tryptophan hydroxylase. For this enzyme to function properly it requires iron in the form of ferrous ions. Assuming an adequate supply of tryptophan, the rate at which this enzyme works determines the amount of melatonin produced. It is a major step in controlling the production of melatonin.

The next step in melatonin production is the conversion of

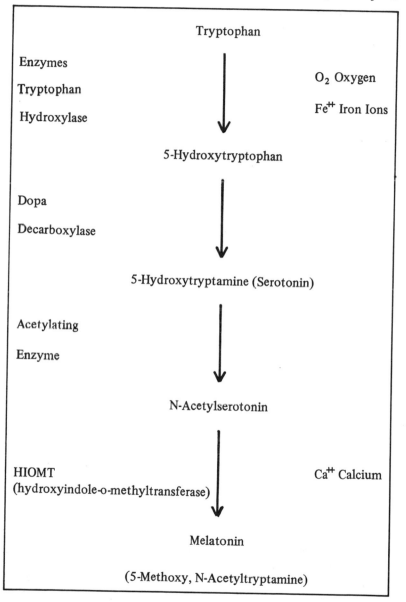

Figure 3: Biosynthesis of melatonin in the pineal gland

5-hydroxytryphtophan into 5-hydroxytryptamine—another hormone, also known as serotonin. The enzyme causing this reaction (dopa decarboxylase) requires a phosphorous-containing chemical for its proper functioning.

Unlike melatonin, serotonin is found in many parts of the body other than the pineal, and it is present in high concentrations in certain other areas of the brain. It is well known that the hallucinogenic drug L.S.D. disrupts brain structures that contain serotonin and it is possible that it is a flood of serotonin in the brain that correlates physically with the hallucinations associated with L.S.D. ingestion. One intriguing report in this context concerns the possible role of the pineal in hallucinatory experiences.

Although animals can't report subjective experiences, they do demonstrate specific behavioural patterns in response to the administration of hallucinogenic drugs. These drugs come in all shapes and sizes and affect various chemicals in various parts of the brain. As we have indicated, serotonin is one of the major chemicals affected by such drugs. It has been demonstrated that animals which have been pinealectomised (had their pineals removed) do not show the expected behavioural responses from hallucinogenic drugs. It may well be, therefore, that we need our pineals to hallucinate.[30]

According to tradition the Buddha received enlightenment (his third eye opened) as he sat beneath a Bo tree. The fruit of the Bo tree contains large amounts of tryptophan and if the Buddha was partaking of this fruit, which is indeed edible, his pineal would have plenty of tryptophan to convert to melatonin. Melatonin administration to human volunteers has been known to produce mood states described as 'elation', so perhaps his illumination owed at least a little to the pineal!

In the pineal, serotonin concentrations undergo a rhythmic twenty-four hour cycle. This cycle seems to be endogenously controlled. In other words, serotonin concentrations follow a day/night cycle in the pineal and this cycle seems to be an intrinsic property of processes within the gland, although it can be synchronized to an extent by changes in day/night length or indeed light/dark cycles. The production of melatonin in the pineal is completed when serotonin is converted into melatonin by the enzyme HIOMT* which requires calcium ions for its proper functioning. Melatonin then passes into the blood stream and is carried round the body.

Like serotonin, melatonin production in the pineal also undergoes cyclic changes. Unlike serotonin, however, this cycle seems to be controlled *extrinsically* by the day/night cycle and is due to changes in the activity of HIOMT.

This final process—the conversion of serotonin into melatonin—takes places in a gland tucked away in the darkness of the centre of the brain. The major factor, however, which determines the rate of this final step is *light*. The amount of light animals (including us) are exposed to appears to determine the amount of melatonin produced by the pineal gland. The third eye responds to light. How?

To answer this question we must digress a little and look at birds, amphibians and fish.

It has been known for many years that the skin colour of animals such as frogs, toads and fish undergoes changes. Sometimes the skin is blanched and at other times dark. Lampreys, for example, become blanched when placed in the dark. If their pineal glands are removed, this no longer happens. Their skin contains a pigment called melanin. When it is concentrated tightly in granules in the skin cells of these animals, they are blanched. Conversely, when it is dispersed in the cells, they become dark.

As early as 1917 it was known that when extracts of pineal glands were fed to frogs and tadpoles, their skin rapidly lightened. It was not until 1958, however, that it was demonstrated that melatonin was responsible for this effect. Indeed the word 'melatonin' is derived from this effect on the pigment melanin, and melatonin is the most potent blanching agent known.

In animals such as these the pineal gland is *directly* responsive to light, and it converts light impulses which impinge on to the gland into nerve impulses. In other words, in these

---

*Hydroxyindole-o-methyl transferase.

animals the pineal gland is truly a third eye showing the characteristic feature of an eye, namely the ability to convert light waves directly into nerve impulses. Like the amphibians, birds too have pineal glands which are directly responsive to light. This fact was elegantly demonstrated in an imaginative study where, by painting the heads of Japanese quail with radio luminous paint, the effects of different wavelengths of light on the pineal could be observed.[15] It was found that direct stimulation of the pineal in quail could be produced by light of long wavelength only.

With one possible exception, which we shall discuss below, it appears that in higher animals stimulation of the pineal gland by light occurs exclusively *indirectly*. Very appropriately, the third eye in mammals is stimulated via the other two.

As we all know, light impinges on our eyes and sets up nerve impulses in our optic nerves which ultimately produce images in our brains. What is not always realized, however, is that some of the nerve impulses in the optic nerves do not travel along to the image-producing centres. Some inquisitive ones take another, rather circuitous route and, after a quick visit to the spinal column, go back into the brain and descend on the pineal gland. When they get there they *inhibit* the production of melatonin by inhibiting the enzyme HIOMT which converts serotonin to melatonin. This point is worth stressing. *Light inhibits the production of melatonin by the pineal gland.*

In mammals, as we have indicated, this is not a direct effect of light on the gland, but an indirect one via the eyes and offshoots of the optic nerves. If the eyes are blind, light does not inhibit melatonin synthesis, at least in adults. In the newly-born things are a little different.

It has been demonstrated that the nerve impulses which end in the pineal originate in the retina of the eye, that is, in the same area as the sight-producing impulses originate. In new-born mammals, however, light can affect the pineal by another pathway, an extra-retinal one. If, for example, baby rats are blinded so that light cannot set up impulses in the retina, the pineal still responds to light. In other words, light affects the pineal by some other route. This effect is evident, however, only in young animals, and in rats it disappears by the age of twenty-seven days.[32]

This effect appears to be mediated by light penetrating through the (unclosed) skulls of these animals directly on to the pineal. If the blinded rats are hooded, their pineals do not respond to light. It seems likely that light could have this effect until the bones which interlink the skull—the fontanelles—are completely fused.

Animal studies have shown that other parts of the brain can potentially be directly stimulated by light of sufficient intensity. The hypothalamus and temporal lobes of animals, for example, can be electrically altered by light. The physiological significance of this, if any, is unknown. [11]

With respect to the intensity of natural light required to affect the pineal, sunlight is easily strong enough; moonlight, however, even at full moon would not appear to be sufficiently intense to produce a major effect.[21]

So in mammals the pineal gland produces melatonin using tryptophan, iron, calcium, phosphorous and other bits and pieces obtained from the diet. It will tick over quite nicely in the dark, producing melatonin by the plenty. In the light, however, production is slowed down, and melatonin levels, both in the pineal and in the blood stream, fall. This effect of light is not apparent in blinded adults, but is apparent in blinded neonates up to a certain age.

We saw from the studies of birds that the pineal was directly sensitive only to light of a certain wavelength; this is also true of mammals (Fig. 4). By exposing rats to light sources of different colour (or wavelength, as colour is determined by wavelength) it has been demonstrated that certain colours are more effective in inhibiting HIOMT activity, and thus melatonin production, than others.[4] Green, for example, is most effective in inhibiting melatonin production by the pineal, red completely ineffective. Blue is fairly effective, yellow less so and ultra-violet has a definite but weak inhibitory action. Other radiations have been investigated in terms of activity on the pineal and earth-strength magnetic fields influence this.

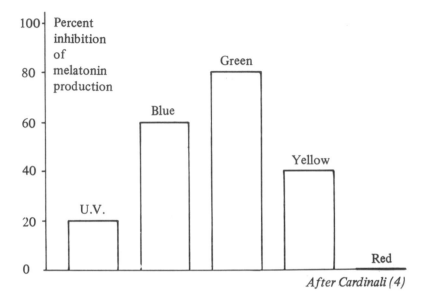

Figure 4: Effect of light colour on pineal activity

It should be borne in mind that just as the effective colours inhibit the production of melatonin by the pineal, so the ineffective colours, such as red, may be considered to be stimulating the pineal's production of melatonin. Darkness too, therefore, might be considered to be a stimulant of the hormone's production. Thus the third eye is most active in the dark, when our other eyes are closed and we are dreaming and watching phantom images.

It has been described how nerve impulses originating in the eyes inhibit pineal function by inhibiting HIOMT activity. It is worth explaining very briefly just how the nerve impulses do this, and to achieve this end we must briefly describe what a nerve impulse is (Fig. 5).

Nerves are not strings or bits of cotton which pull muscles and twitch neurotic eyelids. They are much more sophisticated creatures, being miniature electric cables with inbuilt custom-made chemical amplifiers.

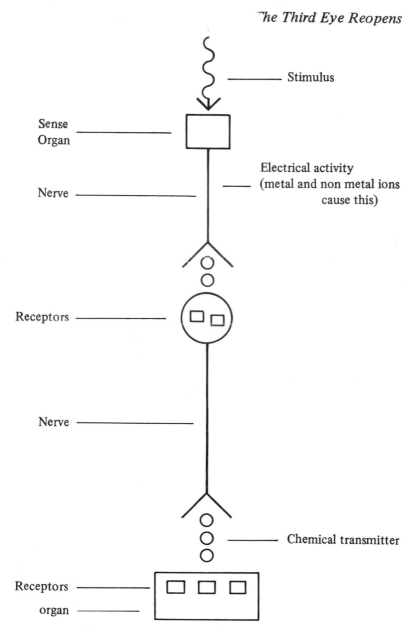

Figure 5: Nerve function

When a stimulus originates in an organ such as an eye or an ear, it sets up a flow of electric current in the nerves associated with it. This is produced and transmitted along the nerve by a flow of positive and negative ions between the inside and outside of the nerve sheath. Because of current leakage this impulse cannot be carried too far without amplificaion, so the body has devised its own delightful system for doing this. At intervals along the nerve there are tiny gaps in the fibres and a chemical is released from the fibre end at one side of the gap by the now weakening impulse. This chemical crosses the gap and stimulates the other end of the fibre, setting up a new, strong impulse. This process is repeated intermittently along the nerve chain until, finally, at the end of the nerve the 'last-lap' impulse arrives. This too releases chemicals from little packets in the nerve ending and these trickle across to the organ being innervated.

In the case of the pineal these nerves (the impulses of which originated in the eye) release a chemical called noradrenaline. It is this chemical which enters the pineal and which, by sticking to certain sensitive sites therein termed receptors, gums up the works of HIOMT and hence melatonin production. The release of this noradrenaline from the nerve endings is very strongly dependent on the presence of calcium. Without calcium the little packets of noradrenaline sit redundant in the nerve endings. The arrival of the nerve impulse allows calcium into the nerve endings, and the packets burst and overflow with noradrenaline which floods the pineal's receptors.

Light, then, stimulates nerves which release noradrenaline. This in turn inhibits HIOMT and melatonin production. In the dark, noradrenaline is not released because these nerves are not active and melatonin production is uninhibited.

Simply, therefore:

Dark —melatonin production
Light—melatonin inhibition

which will bring us back to Eskimos and infertile blind women and later to schizophrenics. Before that, a brief return to

M. Descartes.

The relation between light and pineal function has been established in the past decade or so. It is well represented in the etching illustrated (Fig. 6). This clearly shows light entering the eyes, passing along the optic tracts and impinging on to the pineal which is obviously releasing melatonin which will be inhibited by the light. This etching was made by Descartes and published posthumously in 1664, that is, some three hundred years before this sequence of events was known. Perhaps when in 1640 Descartes made other claims for the pineal, he knew something else that science would take three hundred years to discover.

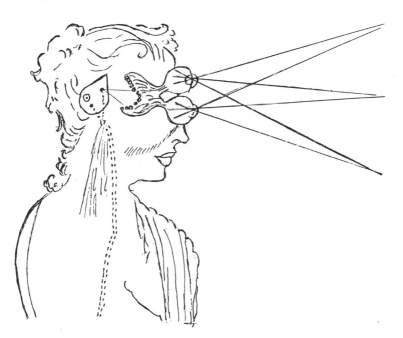

Figure 6: Etching of pineal's position by Descartes.

This figure demonstrates quite clearly light impinging on the eyes and affecting melatonin output from the pineal gland. It is taken from an etching made by Rene Descartes some three hundred years before this effect was discovered.

*   *   *   *   *   *   *   *   *

As a leader to this section, I should like to make a few comments concerning the experimental results described.

The effects described are, unless otherwise stated, attributed to melatonin. It is likely, however, that some of them at least are caused by other pineal hormones, albeit most likely derivatives of melatonin.

Species of animal, dose of melatonin and other factors vary with experiments and hence due caution should be exercised accordingly in interpreting results. It is not valid simply to extrapolate experimental findings from the animal situation to the human one, particularly where a gland is concerned which is so sensitive to photoperiod and hence to animal behavioural patterns as the pineal.

As with any gland, removal of the pineal (pinealectomy) means removal of *all* its products, not just one. However, as melatonin is almost exclusively produced in the pineal, pinealectomy is a very useful tool for looking at the effects of the absence of melatonin in an animal.

Most experiments involving pinealectomy are controlled. Thus pinealectomised animals are compared with 'sham operated' animals, e.g. animals which undergo the same surgical procedure but whose pineals are left intact. This allows for control of effects due to anaesthesia and surgical trauma. Both of these groups can be compared with un-operated control groups if necessary.

Thus, with these qualifications, we can look at the effects melatonin seems to have in mammalian systems.

The most evident effect of melatonin in mammals is its antigonadal activity, i.e. its inhibitory effect on the sexual organs. The effects of melatonin on the sexual organs and the factors in the body which control them are shown in Table 1.

TABLE I [22][23][24]

The effects of melatonin on sexual factors

Melatonin can cause:—

Decreased gonadal weight
Delayed onset of puberty
Suppression of spontaneous or induced ovulation
Decreased ovarian progesterone
Decreased serum follicle stimulating hormone
Decreased serum luteinizing hormone
Increased serum prolactin
Decreased testosterone synthesis
Increased testosterone metabolism in liver
Increased progesterone synthesis
Decreased pituitary luteinizing hormone
Increased pituitary serotonin
Decreased hypothalamic gonadotropin releasing factors
Inhibition of uterine contractions

Despite the fact that most of these effects have yet to be reported in humans, and that in some cases the doses of melatonin producing these effects were what we would term 'unphysiological' (i.e. too high to extrapolate to normal working conditions in the body), there is still an impressive body of evidence to demonstrate the importance of the effect of melatonin on sexual function. It should be noted that the major control of sexual function in mammals is via the pituitary gland which in turn controls the hypothalamus. Melatonin (and hence the pineal) affects both.[14]

In addition to the above observations it is well documented that exposure of male rodents, such as hamsters and rats, to excessive lighting (i.e. increasing their normal photoperiod) causes increased growth of their testicles, and exposure to constant darkness, or significantly decreased photoperiod, produces the opposite effect.[10] Such effects can be reversed by administration of melatonin, implying its role in these processes.

Increased lighting decreases melatonin production by the pineal. Hence it would seem that rodents exposed to constant light do not endure the same degree of antigonadal activity from melatonin, and consequently their reproductive organs enlarge. When kept in constant darkness the opposite apparently happens—increased melatonin output occurs and there is inhibition of testicular growth.

It is not only the gonads which melatonin affects. Other organs are affected as well. Again, species of animal and dosage of melatonin vary from case to case, but the more general effects of melatonin are shown in Table 2.

Once more, allowing for experimental licence, the evidence suggests that there is hardly a system in the body which is not potentially sensitive to the attentions of melatonin. Of particular interest, perhaps, is the fact that melatonin affects pineal function and hence, potentially, its own production.

As we have stressed, one of the most potent activities of melatonin is its antigonadal activity. In summary, we find that in females it can reduce ovarian weight (when given in puberty *or* adulthood), and it can delay vaginal opening time (or the onset of mating behaviour) if repeatedly administered. It can also *prevent* ovulation if administered in a sufficiently high dose. In males it can inhibit growth and functional activity of the testes.

One intriguing aspect of such effects of melatonin is that they may be dependant upon the *age* of the animal at the time of administration of melatonin.[29] For example, not only can melatonin directly affect vaginal opening time in adult animals, but a single injection given during the first two days of life in rats or mice also has an inhibitory action on vaginal opening time *later* in life. Similarly, melatonin administered to rats or mice two days after birth decreases the incidence of oestrus (i.e. ovulation/menstruation) in these species. However, if administered at day 13 after birth, which is still pre-puberty in these animals, these effects are not apparent. (Fig. 7)

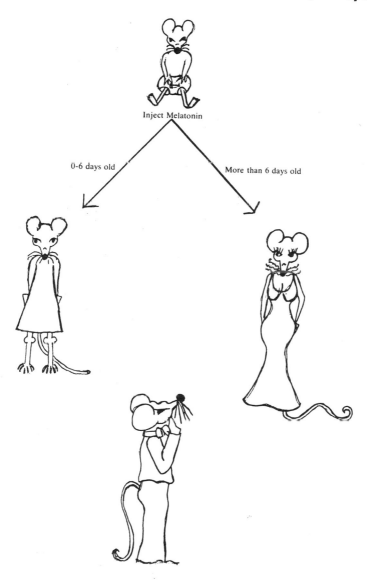

Inject Melatonin

0-6 days old

More than 6 days old

Figure 7: Pre-programming of the delay in onset of oestrus by melatonin

---

TABLE 2 [(22)(23)(24)]

General effects of melatonin

Melatonin:—

> Decreases weight of pituitary
> Increases synthesis of growth hormone
> Decreases weight of thyroid and significantly affects thyroid function
> Decreases steroid production in adrenal glands
> Blocks glucose induced insulin release from pancreas gland
> Inhibits contractions of smooth muscle, e.g. small intestine
> Increases brain content of noradrenaline and serotonin
> Prevents normal diurnal rhythm of serotonin in the pineal
> Increases throxine uptake into the pineal
> Decreases urinary output of oestrogens
> Decreases milk yield (in lactating animals)
> Decreases blood glucose

It seems, therefore, that there is a *specific period after birth* when the animal is sensitive to melatonin in a way which will *subsequently* manifest itself—in this case as a delayed onset of puberty.

The enzyme HIOMT, which produces melatonin from serotonin, is not detectable in new-born rats. It becomes detectable and demonstrates its cyclic activity in response to light/dark changes some six days after birth. This is also the earliest time at which the intrinsic serotonin diurnal cycle becomes apparent.

It would appear, therefore, that in these rodents development of the parts of the brain and body sensitive to melatonin occurs either under gradually increasing concentrations of the hormone or, alternatively, they may develop in the absence of the hormone until it suddenly appears around day six post partum.

We have seen how melatonin given at two days post-natally produced effects which were not apparent when it was given thirteen days post-natally, and that such effects were delayed in onset. In a sense, melatonin appears to *pre-programme* the time of vaginal opening or the degree of oestrus, but the pre-programming can only be done during a certain *critical* period between 0–13 days post-natally. This period, of course, encompasses the time when melatonin is either not being produced by the neonatal pineal or is only being produced at very low levels.

It is not unreasonable, therefore, to postulate the following:

1. When melatonin production by the pineal is normal (around day 6 post-natal in rats), subsequent aspects of sexual behaviour are pre-programmed. In the absence of any interference in this process, normal sexual development of the animal takes place.

2. If, however, the animal is exposed to melatonin before this time, a corresponding alteration in time of sexual maturation and behaviour occurs.

3. The rate of production of melatonin in the neonatal pineal gland can to some extent affect the subsequent development and behaviour of the mature animal.

The above reports have demonstrated that melatonin can affect many of the bits and pieces of the body. The obvious step now is to see how it affects the body *en masse* in terms of behaviour. This implies, of course, looking at the possible mood changes that it may produce.

Due to the significant effect melatonin has on the reproductive system, it would not seem unreasonable to expect it to affect sexual and reproductive behavioural patterns. Experiments to study this have been carried out, not using melatonin *per se* but by using pinealectomised animals and controls as described above. Thus the effects we would observe, if any, would probably (in the pinealectomised animals) be due to *lack* of melatonin (or other pineal hormones).

Baum, in 1968, reported that male rats who were pinealectomised were sexually more precocious than sham-operated control rats. However, despite this earlier interest in the gentler sex when these rats reached adulthood and passed from the precocious passions of adolescence, there was no difference in sexual behaviour between them and the controls.[2] Thus the conclusion was that pinealectomy (at birth) produced definite but short-lived effects on male rats' sexual behaviour in later life.

A more intriguing observation was made by Sampson in 1972 on maternal behaviour of female rats pinealectomised from birth.[26]

The experimental procedure was relatively complex and a simplified version will be given here. In essence, maternal behaviour in pinealectomised and control female rats was compared. Maternal behaviour was assessed by noting how the mothers behaved towards their offspring, how tidy they kept their nests, how much time they spent out of the nest, how careful they were in retrieving offspring removed from the nest, how carefully they fed their offspring and how many offspring lived to weaning.

In all cases where there were differences between the groups, the pinealectomised animals were rated less effective mothers than the controls. The most pronounced effect was evident in the response of the pinealectomised animals to their offspring in the first twenty-four hours after birth. Only within the pinealectomised group did the mothers fail to retrieve all their pups into the nest by two hours after birth, and one of the (fourteen) animals ignored her litter completely. Perhaps the most significant measure of maternal care is survival of the offspring. Twenty-three offspring died in the pinealectomised animal group compared with four in a 'sham operated' group.

The conclusion reached from this work was that the probable cause of the high fatality rate in the pinealectomised group was the poor care of pups in the first twenty-four hours after birth, as after this the pinealectomised animals gradually became more maternal. Hence it was felt that the effects of pinealectomy on maternal behaviour might be limited to a period immediately after birth. Thus, as with the male rats' sexual behaviour, it was felt that the absence of the pineal, and of melatonin, had a delayed onset effect on maternal behaviour which was relatively short-lived.

There is evidence to suggest that the pineal, or melatonin, can produce other behavioural effects in animals. For example, it probably affects the movement or activity of animals and also their feeding habits.[3] However, as movement and feeding in animals such as rats follows a fairly precise daily rhythm, as does pineal activity, this is difficult to establish with certainty. One study, however, strongly suggests that melatonin (or constant darkness) administered to rats produces a rapid and significant increase in their consumption of alcohol, once they've acquired the taste for it. A point perhaps on which to ponder![12]

When we go from rats and mice to men we find that melatonin continues to exert quite dramatic effects. In humans it can apparently cause a sedative effect, increase EEG* alpha activity and synchronization, make sleep easily induced, increase REM[+] sleep cycles, cause vivid dreams and produce feelings of elation and hallucinations.[24] It also seems that extracts of the pineal gland (but not necessarily melatonin alone) can exert beneficial effects in schizophrenic patients.[9]

These effects have been observed after administration of melatonin to human subjects, usually by intravenous injection. There is indirect evidence that other actions of melatonin observed in animal studies may also be extrapolated to the human situation. For example, it is well documented that subjects who have had malignant disease of the pineal have demonstrated sexual precocity. So, too, studies on human tissues in isolation have borne out observations made on animal tissue. For example, human uterine contractions are every bit as well inhibited by melatonin as are contrac-

---

(+), (*) : defined below

tions of the rat uterus.[13] Now let us have a brief digression into sleep and dreams.

An EEG (electroencephalogram) is, of course, a machine used for recording the electrical activity of the brain. Although it records total brain electrical activity, within this it produces reproducible and definite wave patterns which correlate with specific mental states. There are a number of these wave patterns, but only a few need concern us here.

If we relax and close our eyes while attached to an EEG, rhythms appear with a frequency of about ten cycles per second. These are called 'alpha rhythms', and show that we are vigilant yet relaxed with eyes closed. Alpha waves disappear if we open our eyes, are 'aroused' or become sleepy.

As we pass into sleep the waves become larger and slower until in deep sleep they reach one to three cycles per second. Occasional bursts of faster waves called spindles, however, intrude on the slow waves of our slumbers as do other less frequent ripples of mentation. For about one to two hours in the night, the large slow waves and spindles of deep sleep are interrupted by low voltage EEG patterns; simultaneously the eyes make rapid conjugate movements termed, appropriately enough, rapid eye movements (REMs). This type of sleep is termed REM sleep and it seems that most, if not all, or our dreaming is done during this period. The characteristic REM sleep waves on the EEG, then, can tell us when a person is dreaming. This enables us to allow him to sleep, but not to dream, simply by waking him up each time REM sleep waves appear on the EEG. If we do this to someone for long enough they tend, apparently, to go temporarily mad.

Two examples from Dement (1970) illustrate this point well.[6] After fifteen nights of REM sleep deprivation, one subject abruptly underwent a personality change in which his high moral standards suddenly reverted to a desire to seek out the 'sexiest entertainment available.' Another subject changed abruptly after fourteen nights of REM sleep deprivation and became paranoid and autistic; this particular experiment was terminated to avoid a 'full-blown psychosis'.

Whilst these two cases are relatively extreme, they show

what *can* happen with REM deprivation or, alternatively, when you stop people dreaming. Interestingly enough, once you allow such subjects to return to normal sleep patterns, they make up the REM sleep they have lost. Further, as such experiments progress, it becomes more and more difficult to waken a person during the REM phase, indeed keeping them awake at all becomes progressively more difficult. It is as if, when you are kept from dreaming, some chemical builds up in the brain urging it to sleep and dream.

For some years such a natural sleep-producing chemical has been postulated as existing in the body. It has now apparently been discovered. In the pineal gland.

Melatonin not only produces increased REM cycles in our sleep and enriches our dreams with vividity, it also releases from the pineal a substance called vasotocin.

Chemically, vasotocin is quite unlike melatonin; it does, however, share the ability of melatonin to cause sedation or, to be more precise, sleep. A millionth of a billionth of a gram of vasotocin injected into a cat will send it to sleep in five minutes.[25] This makes vasotocin the most potent substance known to be capable of inducing sleep. The release of vasotocin into the cerebrospinal fluid of man during the night possibly causes sleep. Darkness releases melatonin, melatonin releases vasotocin, vasotocin causes sleep. While not necessarily true of rats, it may be that humans can go to sleep simply by closing their eyes and shutting out light.

It is possible that some apparent effects of melatonin are produced by its release of vasotocin. One of the properties of the latter is that it suppresses REM sleep. (This fact could explain why melatonin has been reported both to increase *and* decrease REM sleep frequency—by stimulating it directly and suppressing it indirectly by release of vasotocin.)

All in all, then, we see that melatonin and its stablemate vasotocin are extremely interesting substances indeed. The former appears both to be able to pre-programme behaviour and to have a multitude of direct effects on bodily systems. The latter appears to give us a chemical link with the world of sleep and dreams.

Therefore, in view of these diverse effects, particularly of melatonin, it should now be possible to appreciate the not unlikely connections between Eskimos ceasing menstruation in winter, superovulation in summer time, the relative sterility of congenitally blind women, and the regulation of menstrual cycles by bedside lamps!

As we have established, melatonin is antigonadotrophic. It inhibits reproductive processes, both directly and via the hormones that control them. It also seems to modify behaviour. In other words, as long as the pineal secretes melatonin in its twenty-four hour cycle, there will be a degree of inhibition of reproductive function and possibly also of instinctive sexual behaviour. The major controlling factor in pineal production of melatonin is *light*.

In winter, when Eskimos are exposed to constant darkness, they constantly secrete the antigonadal substance melatonin; they stop menstruating and lose their libido. Congenitally blind women are similarly in constant darkness; they tend not to ovulate.

Conversely, expose people to light, inhibit melatonin (thus preventing its inhibitory action on reproductive function), and we get more ovulation and hence conception in summer, and regularization of menstrual cycles in women exposed to the light of bedside lamps at the ovulatory phase of the cycle.

Now one realizes that such broad generalizations require some qualification, and there are obviously a number of factors such as genetic make-up, dietary factors, environmental conditions and so on, which will affect the response of each individual. However, such factors will simply complicate individual observation and mean that we have to look at large numbers of subjects to obtain an insight into the underlying factors at work.

I feel it is completely reasonable to assume that in the situations described above the major underlying factor is the relationship between light and pineal function. Indeed it is difficult to see what else it could be.

We shall return to the pineal gland later in an attempt to

understand what role it may play in our physical and mental experiences and development in relation to our environment in the widest sense of the word. Later, too, we shall look at its possible role in schizophrenia, using this as an example of a model situation for the possible effects cosmic influences have on us at birth in relation to our subsequent development. As we progress through the ensuing chapters it is worth bearing a few major points in mind concerning this gland.

The pineal gland exerts actions which are perhaps of major significance in determining our behaviour. It secretes substances which may strictly bind us to the dictates of the physical world and yet lose us to the irrationalities of the mind wandering in dreams. It is responsive to sun and season, light and dark. It ebbs and flows in cycles of chemical waves. It is an ancient eye watching in the darkness, perhaps the major controller of all body cycles. It may pre-programme some of our behaviour, possibly winding us up like alarm clocks.

Ingesting metals, spilling fluids; the crown chakra, the seat of the soul, has only just begun to reveal itself.

CHAPTER II

Lights and cycles in The Sky

We are told that, for some as yet obscure reason, when babies are born who will subsequently become highly successful scientists, athletes, doctors or executives, the planet Mars decides either to be rising in the East or setting in the West of their place of birth. It does not care to occupy any other position. With more artistic types, however, Mars neither rises nor sets about them, but apparently chooses to *avoid* such positions in the sky. Jupiter, Saturn and the Moon appear also to have similar prejudices for people who will become eminent in certain professions. These observations, reported by Michell Gauquelin, when statistically analysed are scientific *fact*.[16] They seem also, of course, completely irrational.

Maki Takata demonstrated that a protein in the blood known as albumin can be made to precipitate out of serum by the addition of a certain chemical to the serum. The rate of this precipitation is constant amongst men, though it varies with the menstrual cycle in women. Because of this it could be used to test what point a woman had reached in her menstrual cycle. In 1938 the rate of this reaction suddenly became unpredictable both in males and females. It was demonstrated that variations in the activity of the Sun corresponded with changes in this precipitation (or flocculation) index of albumin. It seemed that a change in the activity of the Sun registered in Man's albumin. This effect of the Sun on albumin flocculation shows an increase when the Earth moves into line with a group of sunspots. It is reduced when the Moon eclipses the Sun. Hence the Moon shields us from it. There is an increased effect about fifteen minutes *prior* to sunrise, so the body, the 'human sundial', anticipates this effect.[33]

If you take the relative movement of the Sun round the Earth and consider it as inscribing a circular belt of 360°, it has been claimed that a child born every third degree of the Sun's movement is 37 per cent more likely to contract polio than a child born in the two intermediary degrees.[2]

In a study of 37,000 couples and their children, it was reported that planetary positions relative to the Earth at the times of the parents' birth, were significantly related to the positions of the planets at the time of their offsprings' birth. If the children's births were induced artificially this effect was reported as being not evident.[17]

It is well established that human beings, like other living organisms, exhibit an electrical potential across the body surface and that they are surrounded by an electrical field. This potential undergoes changes coincident with seasonal changes and with the phases of the Moon. Patients who are mentally ill reportedly demonstrate changes in potential which are proportional to the assessed severity of their mental illness.[29]

The rate of precipitation from aqueous solution of the chemical bismuth oxychloride is variable. It alters from day to day and demonstrates a cyclical pattern throughout the year with minima occurring in March and, to a lesser extent, in September. This cycle varies with latitude and is affected by magnetic disturbance. It also correlates quite dramatically with the activity of sunsports. If the experimental system measuring the rate of precipitation is enclosed, and thus shielded by copper plating, this cyclic process disappears and the precipitate forms at a constant rate. This observation was made and carefully investigated by Professor G. Piccardi, and described by him in 1959.[27]

It is reported that there is a remarkable correlation between heart attacks, solar activity and peaks of magnetic disturbances. Such magnetic disturbances can be anticipated and, by taking appropriate measures prior to their occurrence, a considerable decrease in death rate due to heart attacks has apparently been achieved. It seems that relatively few heart attacks occur during periods of low solar activity.[28]

It has been claimed that mistletoe has been successfuly used to treat cancer. A prerequisite for success, however, is apparently the time when the mistletoe is collected. When the sap from mistletoe is allowed to diffuse up sheets of filter paper, it produces patterns and forms which can be made visible by staining. Such patterns have been demonstrated to be quite insensitive to alterations in ambient weather conditions. Extra-terrestial events however, particularly eclipses, apparently quite dramatically alter their shape.[15]

When a solution of iron sulphate is mixed with a solution of silver nitrate, a chemical reaction occurs causing silver to precipitate out of solution. When lead nitrate is added to the mixed solutions it slows the process, making it easier to measure the rate at which the precipitation of silver occurs. The rate thus measured is relatively constant. When Mars and Saturn come into conjunction (eclipse); precipitation ostensibly stops.[21]

Planets move at different orbital speeds, hence the faster ones catch up on the slower ones. Venus, for example, moves faster than Saturn and will approach it (apply), conjunct it (eclipse), then pass it (separate). In analogy with the Doppler effect—where sound approaching you seems loud and stressed (as wavelength shortens) and sound passing you seems relaxed and relatively quiet—planets applying might be considered to be 'stressful' and those separating 'relaxed'. In a study involving almost one thousand nonagenarians it was reported that there was an immensely significant number of separating planets at their time of birth. In other words, the presence of lots of separating planets at your time of birth increases the chance that you'll live to be a nonagenarian.[1]

Dr. A. Hoffer reported that depressives were unmistakably more severely ill in March, unlike neurotics who show exacerbation of their condition in January and July. This observations on mental state and association with month or season is reminiscent of the observations made concerning seasonal peak births of schizophrenics. It is interesting that Dr. Hoffer reported schizophrenics 'remarkably insensitive' to the periodic variations which so affected neurotics and depressives.

*   *   *   *   *   *   *   *   *

It should be evident that in all these situations (which, almost without exception, have been reported by respected and qualified people) there is a common link: the implication that extra-terrestrial phenomena can affect matters of varied types on Earth. At this point, therefore, it may be opportune to take a brief look at the Sun, its showers, the Moon, the planets and people, and then at some mysterious cycles uncovered in the University of Harvard.

The Sun emits an enormous number of waves which encompass the range of the electromagnetic spectrum. Its activity is not constant and this bombardment of radiation oscillates with solar vagaries. There are, however, *some* defined regular cycles associated with solar activity. For example, the Sun, like the Earth, revolves around its own axis. The period of this revolution is twenty-seven days. Thus it sprays out its stream of particles and waves like some enormous beacon and, to an extent, the intensity of this energy stream on earth will be dependent on the phase of its twenty-seven-day cycle of axial rotation.

The most dramatic cycle of solar activity, however, is the sunspot cycle. Sunspots are hugh blemishes on the solar surface which explosively stir up dramatic magnetic whirlwinds which reach raging peaks of activity before disappearing as suddenly as they arrived. Sunspot activity follows a cycle of 11.1 years. Every eleven years the Sun begins positively to sprinkle with sunspots and like some celestial acne the spots spread and erupt. Soon, however, the process subsides and the number of sunspots decreases and falls, to peak again eleven years later.

Why sunspots exhibit this eleven-year cycle has been subject to some debate. It has been suggested, for example, that sunspots are related to the movement of Jupiter which takes 11.86 years to orbit the Sun. It has also been suggested that the Earth itself affects sunspot activity, particularly when in conjunction with another planet such as Venus. Most interesting in this context, however, are the relationships established by Professor E. R. Dewey which were published in 1968.[14]

Sunspots are magnetized entities and they normally occur in pairs. Dewey reasoned that because in one eleven-year cycle sunspots at the north of the Sun lead, and those in the south follow, while the opposite occurs in the next eleven-year cycle, a true cycle of sunspot activity would be approximately twenty-two years (22.22 years precisely). By using some fairly sophisticated mathematical techniques Dewey demonstrated that sunspot activity was coincident with conjunctions occurring between any of the planets Saturn, Uranus, Jupiter and Pluto.

This observation by Dewey correlates with the view of the meteorologist J. M. Mitchell, who has suggested that water shortage in California and Great Plains snow deficits may follow roughly a twenty-year sunspot-related drought cycle.[25] Such conclusions relating cosmic events to earthly ones have never pleased meteorologists or astronomers for reasons best known to themselves. However we are far from knowing all the secrets of the Sun; apparently we don't even know why it shines!

For many years it was believed that the Sun shone due to energy released by fusion of hydrogen nuclei in the Sun's core. Such a concept is incompatible with the fascinating reports generated independently by astronomers from Britain and the U.S.S.R. that the Sun beats 'like a gigantic heart' with a 'pulse' rate of one beat every two hours forty minutes.[31] These observations have led to the sad admission that it is quite possible that the actual physical process which causes the Sun to shine may be one quite unknown to science.

This 'heart beat' of the Sun makes an aesthetically neat complement to the rhythmic 'call' of the Earth. This 'call' is an immense 'shout' which the Earth screams out precisely sixty-nine times per day. The Earth-ionosphere cavity acts as a natural resonator and our planet resounds once every twenty minutes, fifty seconds.[35] Hence Sun and Earth have diurnal rhythmic beats like living things.

For some years now it has been recognized that people are particularly sensitive to a preponderance of charged atoms (ions) in the atmosphere. When there is a preponderance of positive ions people become depressed, anxious and irritable, whereas a surfeit of negative ions makes people refreshed and active. Drs. Krueger and Sulman have indicated that positive ions produce this effect by increasing body levels of serotonin (5-hydroxytryptamine), the chemical forerunner of melatonin.

The most infamous example of positive ions disturbance is that of the *foehn,* the ill wind which strikes the populace of Switzerland, Austria and Bavaria. It spreads, if not quite plague and pestilence, at least depression and increased suffering and mortality. Swiss judges have often ruled that *foehn* winds constitute extenuating circumstances in serious crimes, including murder.[4] Apparently the *foehn,* and other similar hot dry winds, known variously as *sharav, sirocco* and *harmattan,* make the average person experience pressure behind the eyes and produces a general sensation of a 'foggy brain'. The ubiquitous sensation spread by the *foehn* has been beautifully captured by N. L. Bello in an article he wrote about it. 'The *foehn,*' he wrote, 'had no iffeck on my brainn or the way my finggger hit the kies of the typerighter.[4]

Not only ionic changes, but other changes in the atmosphere can ostensibly cause alterations in human behaviour. Fluctuations in atmospheric pressure, temperature, humidity and electromagnetic status have been reported as producing effects varying from increased incidence of strokes to self-inflicted injuries. When we appreciate that the weather and hence atmospheric conditions can be affected by the Moon, it is not surprising to find that, as indicated above, the electrical potential of the body varies with lunar phases, or that 'rape, robbery, assault, burglary, larceny and theft, auto-theft, offences against family and children, drunkenness and disorderly conduct occurred significantly more frequently during the full moon phase than at any other time of the year.'[34] Nor is it surprising that some people still look to the 'stars' for explanations.

In an article in *Nature* Begleman et al. indicated that there was an impressive array of evidence suggesting that solar activity influences the Earth's climate through effects of the solar wind. It was suggested that the solar wind 'blew' cosmic particles on to Earth and altered the ionization balance in the lower atmosphere.

D. A. Bradley and E. G. Bowen have demonstrated that the Moon causes widespread changes in atmospheric precipitation as well as having a significant effect on incoming meteorite rate [6] [7]

We know well, of course that the Moon rhythmically causes the rise and fall of the oceans twice a day. Less well known is the fact that it also produces tides in the atmosphere. This 'breathing' of the ocean of air surrounding us has been well described by Chapman.[10]

The Sun also produces tides in the atmosphere and affects the oceans' tides, accounting for the spring and neap tides. In the atmosphere the Sun tide is between fifteen to twenty times stronger than the lunar one. Chapman describes these thus:

> To use a musical analogy, the Moon tide and Sun tide correspond to two pure notes of different pitch and intensity. The Moon tide note has one vibration in 12 hours 25 minutes, the Sun tide note has a slightly higher 'pitch'—one vibration every 12 hours ... the Sun tide is a barely audible monotone and the Moon tide is a muted note which can be heard only by a specially attuned ear.

One special feature of this Moon tide is that it causes a waxing and waning of the cosmic ray showers falling on to the Earth.

In view of such facts and in view of the established effects of ion imbalance already referred to, it is becoming sensible rather than credulous to associate lunar and solar activity with human behaviour.

Other things fly down from the heavens to us, of course, the most notable being meteorites and cosmic rays. The influx of meteorites is (as we have mentioned) affected by the Moon. She must have been in a particularly cynical frame of mind in 1908, therefore, when a (probable) meteorite of gigantic proportions hit the region of Tunguska in Russia. This meteorite devastated 1,500 square miles of forest, and it has been discovered that genetic mutation in the local vegetation has been racing ahead, ignoring the normal conservative constraints of Nature since.[32]

Much less conspicuous than meteorites, but equally capable of interfering with genes, and in turn being interfered with by the Moon, are cosmic rays. These energetic and fascinating particles appear to originate from supernovas (exploding stars in our own galaxy) and not, as had once been suspected, from other galaxies.

In 1951 J. H. Nelson published the first of a series of articles claiming relationships between planets and electromagnetic phenomena.[26]* Nelson, in a retrospective survey, claimed that magnetic storms, which cause radio disturbance, followed patterns which correlated with the angles the planets made relative to the Sun (Fig. 9). Most magnetic storms were found to occur when two or more planets were in conjunction (0°) or opposition (180°) to the Sun. Disturbance—*free* fields were obtained when the planets formed 60° and 120° angles to the Sun. To quote from an article which

---

*Nelson has undeniably demonstrated a relation between planets and electromagnetic phenomena in studies carried out over many years since 1951. Some of his earlier work however was not as precise and accurate as his later. I use his earlier work to describe his findings nonetheless as it is simpler and amply makes the essential points of his more sophisticated studies.

appeared in the *New York Times,* '. . . the planets and the Sun share in a cosmic electrical-balance mechanism that extends a billion miles from the centre of the solar system. The Sun-field stretches far, and in a sense we are *in* the Sun.'[31]

It would appear that the planets do not confine their attentions solely to electromagnetic radiation either. Dr. R. Tomaschek carried out a statistical analysis of 134 major earthquakes. His findings indicated that, although the positions of the Sun and Moon relative to Earth were unimportant in this context, the positions of the planets, particularly Jupiter, Uranus and Pluto, *were* significant.*

" . . . the Moon tide and the Sun tide correspond to pure notes of different pitch."

"The Sun tide is a barely ' audible monotone and the Moon tide is a muted note which can be heard only by a specially attuned ear."
(Chapman 1956)

Figure 8: Moon tide and Sun tide

---

*Although these findings have been subject to criticism there does seem to be good evidence linking planetary movements and earthquakes. For a review see Dean 1977.[13]

In the book *The Jupiter Effect,* J. R. Gribbin and S. H. Plagemann indicate a possible lunar correlation with earthquakes as implied in the minor, but statistically significant, observation that tides serve as triggers of earthquakes.

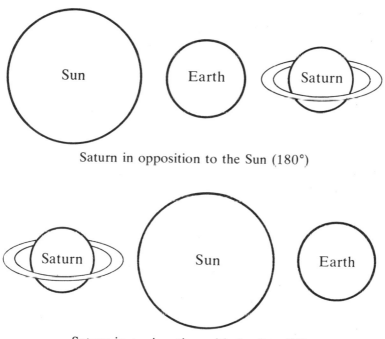

Saturn in opposition to the Sun (180°)

Saturn in conjunction with the Sun (0°)

Figure 9: Planetary aspects.

The planets, therefore, appear to exert at least some control over the bombardment of celestial waves and particles which stream on to the Earth and they may well affect other physical phenomena such as earthquakes, perhaps by gravitational effects. In this latter context it is worth mentioning an observation made by M. Allais in 1954.[3]

41

Allais was observing the period of oscillation of a pendulum during the total solar eclipse of 1954. At the exact moment of eclipse the oscillation of the pendulum abruptly altered. The Moon in some way had screened us from a part of solar attraction. How this could occur is not known. Apparently, however, it did.

In view of the existing evidence, to reject the possibility of extra-terrestrial factors affecting events on Earth is nothing short of ridiculous. Where this attitude prevails, it is reminiscent of the attitude of Galileo's contemporaries to his discovery of the moons of Jupiter. Because they couldn't rationally accept the concept, one of them wouldn't even look through his telescope to see for himself.

It is remarkable that aspects of the behaviour of the Sun, Moon and planets correlate with, and probably cause, at least some events on Earth. They also demonstrate a property which manifests itself on Earth, that of cyclic behaviour. Planets have specific periods of time which they take to orbit the Sun, or the Earth if you look at them from here. Venus, for example, takes 225 days, Mars 1.8 years and so on. They also show cyclical *synodic* periods with respect to one another, i.e. times when they recurrently occupy the same position in the heavens relative to one another. The synodic period for the Moon lying in opposition to the Sun (full moon), for example, is one month, and for Saturn conjuncting Mars about two years.

Whether or not such cycles have any relevance to cycles on Earth is yet to be fully established: though at least in some cases it *would* seem possible because the synodic cycle of some planets, as we have seen, correlates with sunspot activity. Either way, earthly cycles are nothing short of being fascinatingly ordered events of Nature whose origins at present are for the most part obscure.

Professor E. Huntington of Harvard University led a team of researchers who began what was probably the first systematic study of cycles in the 1920s. It would appear that, as much to the surprise of his research group as to anyone else, cycles appeared everywhere they looked. It should be stressed that the cycles these and subsequent workers have found are *true* cycles and not just absurd manifestations of chance. The most convincing evidence in support of this fact is the recurrence of the most unlikely cycles dead on time, time after time. The number and variety of cycles found is astonishing.

It would appear that a number of these cycles may well correlate in one way or another with the solar cycle in general and the sunspot cycle in particular. Where cycles are close to, but not quite in phase with, the solar cycles, it has been postulated that there is a common cause behind both the solar and the other cycles but no direct causal relation between the two.

For example, if we look at the solar cycle we find that correlations exist between solar activity and mining disasters, road accidents, mental depression, suicides, punishment of schoolchildren, admissions to psychiatric hospitals, wars, population movements, epidemics and changes in ruling political parties.[12]

If we turn our attention to the Moon we find that the lunar cycle is apparently correlated with the growth of plants, aggression, menstruation, mental illness, murder, animal activity, earthquakes, haemorrhages and suicides.[22] [34]

Cycles of one sort or another have been found in the realms of economics, agriculture, meteorology, human behaviour, animal behaviour, geophysics and anywhere else you care to look. So again it must be stressed that the distribution of 'cycle' periods is not random, i.e. most authenticated cycles, while quite diverse in nature, show the same or similar periods. Thus we can reasonably accept that cyclic phenomena are meaningful and not coincidental.

Cycles have also been observed in the number of grasshoppers hopping about, the number of successful suicides carried out, the price of butter, the incidence of haemorrhages during surgery, the sale of stocks and shares, the incidence of heart attacks, the price of pig iron, the number of wars and so on and on and on.[12] Note that what we are saying here is that these things occur in a *cyclical* way, that is, they show regular periodic fluctuations. This suggests a harmony in things as diverse as grasshoppers and stocks and shares which causes them to follow a rhythm, even though that rhythm may be difficult to detect and even more difficult to explain.

As an illustration of this point it is notable that there is a 9.6 year cycle evident in the size of salmon catches in Canada, the width of tree rings, and cotton prices in the United States. Thus for some reason the period of 9.6 years is significant in the context of salmon, tree growth and cotton prices. Cycles also tend to occur in a certain harmonic period usually in progressions of twos or threes, but *not* however in progressions of fives or sevens. (For example, a cycle of nine years encloses three three-year cycles.) Certain periods do not apparently demonstrate any cycles at all. 10.6 years, for example, is apparently a cycleless period.

The cycles which have probably attracted most attention are the twenty-four hour, or circadian, cycles which the body undergoes in concert with night and day. Twenty-four hour cycles can be seen at every level: at the level of the tissues and organs and at the level of the whole animal. For example, the volume of a cell nucleus shows a regular variation over the twenty-four hour period.[30] It swells and shrinks, reaching maxima and minima of volume at specific times of the twenty-four hours. Body temperature, heart rate, ability to respond to stimulation, output of urine and sleep-wake patterns all correspond to a twenty-four hour periodic cycle as do many, many other biological phenomena.[30] There are a large number of excellent reviews of biological cycles available and the interested reader should consult these for detailed discussion.[23]

It is now accepted that the circadian rhythm in the body's functioning is ostensibly of two distinct types: an endogenous rhythm—one that is controlled by an *internal* biological 'clock'—and an exogenous rhythm—one that is controlled by an *external* 'clock'. An example of the former type, the supposedly internal body clock, is the level of production of serotonin in the pineal gland. Pineal serotonin levels follow a twenty-four hour cycle which in rats are maximal during the day. Now although this rhythm can be synchronized by external factors and even altered by them to an extent, it will always follow a more or less regular twenty-four hour pattern which is apparently programmed in some way into the gland. The activity of the enzyme HIOMT, however, and thus the production of melatonin in the pineal, follows (as we discussed in Chapter I) an *externally* controlled twenty-four hour cycle. Thus melatonin production follows a regular twenty-four hour cycle and this cycle is determined by the light/dark cycle; it is simply a twenty-four hour cycle because that is the day/night length. Unlike the melatonin cycle, the serotonin cycle would continue unimpeded in constant light or constant dark. Thus it would appear to be truly an internal cycle and, one of the many where the body emulates the period of rotation of the Earth, apparently quite independently of it.

At the grosser level it is evident that the sleep-wake cycle (for most of us a twenty-four hour one) could be either *external* or *internal.* Studies have been carried out to test this cycle, and the results suggest that, even in a constantly illuminated environment, people organize their sleep-wake cycle more or less around the twenty-four hour day. Hence this would suggest that sleep, at least partially, is an internally controlled rhythm, something consistent with our discussion of vasotocin in the first chapter.

We are, of course, making the assumption here that being isolated from light-dark changes removes us from the 'stimulus' of the twenty-four hour cycle. In other words, we assume that *seeing* night-day cues, being directly exposed to them, determines our diurnal rhythm. This may not be the case. Indeed there is evidence to suggest that animals and humans still respond to night and day cycles, or more precisely Sun-Moon cycles, when they are as isolated from them as is physically possible.

There have been a number of studies to demonstrate this fact, but none so pleasing as the celebrated ones of the fiddler crabs, the oysters and the Moon. These studies have often

Sleep
Urine flow
Electricity levels
Pulse rate
Respiration
Blood pressure
Drug metabolism
Drug activity
Hormone levels
Allergies
Mortality

Figure 10: Some factors in humans demonstrating circadian rhythm

been cited, not because they are the only ones of their kind, but because of their elegance. Hence I make no apology for citing them again.

Professor F. Brown demonstrated that the fiddler crab *(uca pugnax)* changed colour in harmony with its environment and in particular in its relationship to the position of the Moon. The obvious conclusion would be that as the moonlight (which, of course, is reflected sunlight) changed with the change in the Moon's phase, so its effect on the crabs' colour pigments would alter the colour of the animals. Obviously, therefore, if the animal were placed in a darkened room, isolated from the Moon, it should stop this Moon-linked colour change. It didn't Enclosed in dark rooms, isolated from moonlight, the crabs continued faithfully to follow the lunar cycle.[8]

Oysters follow a tidal rhythm, opening and closing in concert with the tides. They open at the time the tide brings in their food and close when it removes it. Brown removed twelve specimens of an oyster *(ostrea virginica)* 1,000 miles away from their home by the seaside to his laboratory. For a week or two the oysters optimistically continued opening and closing at their normal feeding times; then they gave up. Progressively they altered their rhythm so that they opened at the time the tide *would* have reached them at their new location. In other words they gave up their old rhythm and began to open and close in relation to the Moon's position at their new home.[9] These experiments were well controlled, and it has to be accepted that in some way oysters, like fiddler crabs, can close their 'eyes' to moonlight yet still respond to lunar cycles. Similar lunar effects have been reported in terms of behaviour in other plant and animal species.

Supporting the possibility that the Moon can affect behavioural patterns in humans is the observation that a blind person isolated from all cues to the twenty-four hour solar cycle responded, in terms of behaviour, to the longer lunar cycle of 24.9 hours.

Such information on biological cycles has, and is, made use of in contemporary medicine and, despite logistical problems, it may prove to be of very significant use in therapeutics.

Certain drugs are very much more effective at certain times of the day.[11] Hence administration of a drug at the most propitious time of the day may mean that a significant decrease in dosage may be administered yet the same effect be produced. If the drug is very expensive or is very toxic (e.g. anti-cancer agents), such a procedure may well be worthwhile adopting.

Values for various physiological parameters such as blood pressure, heart rate and so on, vary drastically with time of day. Blood pressure, pulse rate and heart output all decrease at night and Bondy has given a good description of how such parameters vary during the day.[5] Once more the question remains to be answered as to whether some of these particular cyclic changes are related to cosmological events.

Later, we shall address ourselves further to the subject of how celestial events involving the Sun, Moon, the planets and cosmic radiation can affect us. It is, however, worth making an important comment on the phenomena described so far

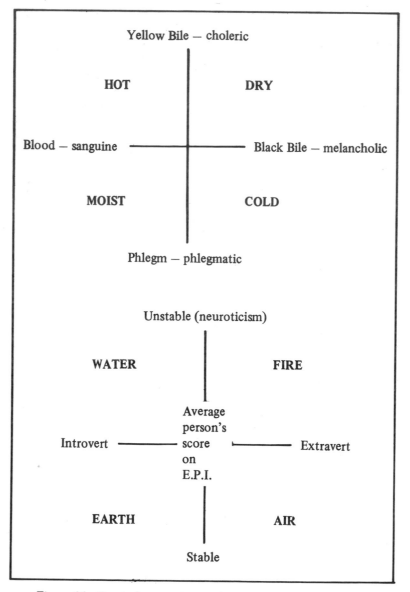

Figure 11: Classical compared with contemporary personality classification.

in this chapter. It should be evident that they can more or less be divided into two distinct categories: one in which a rational scientific explanation is most likely to exist, e.g. an association between planetary groupings and radio interference by magnetic storms; and another where this is not the case, e.g. people born with more separating aspects between planets apparently living longer.

It is as if we have one set of phenomena which is capable of description by accepted physical laws and processes, and another set which is not, This latter set, if valid, would seem to require acausal explanations. This is not necessarily the case, as we may simply be living in ignorance of a number of physical forces which produce these effects. On the other hand, the theoretical framework exists to handle acausality, if it must be handled, as we shall discuss in the next chapter. Before this, however, let us pay a visit to the Greeks and thence to some of the most exciting studies carried out in this area which links us and the Earth with what's around us.

According to the ancient Greeks the human body contained four humours, Bile, Blood, Phlegm and Black Bile. This meaning of 'humour' is well described by Hippocrates in his text *On the Nature of Man*. Basically it was held that healthy individuals contained the humours in more or less balanced proportions. There was always likely to be some imbalance, however, even in relatively healthy specimens, and such imbalances allowed one or other humour to dominate an individual's constitution. Consequently people were classified according to which humour dominated their personality, and four specific types or categories of individuals were recognized: bilious, sanguine, choleric or melancholic (lit. 'black bile').

Each humour was associated with a specific element—fire, earth, air or water—and with a specific season of the year. The coldest humour, Phlegm, for example, was associated with water and winter. Such an association is not difficult to form empirically. Streaming eyes and noses, for example, appeared in the populace in winter time. Blood was associated with air and springtime, and it was during the relative warmth and moisture of spring that Blood increased in power over the other humours, giving rise to nose-bleeds and haemorrhages.

With the onset of the hot dry summer, the Bile became stored up and people became bilious, their skins often turned yellow and fevers prevailed. In addition to the falling leaves, autumn, season of the Earth, brought the dreaded Black Bile to the fore, leaving melancholic types particularly, stoically awaiting the return of Phlegm.

Today such ideas seem quaint. Despite their obvious limitations, however, we mustn't ignore the major intellectual advance made by the Greeks in attempting empirically to classify things into a meaningful system. Oddly enough, although we no longer have individuals constructed of Blood, Bile, Black Bile and Phlegm, we do still have individuals constructed of very similar things. In one sense at least, these new concepts correlate with the Greek associations of fire, earth, air and water or, to be more precise, with positivity (fire and air) and negativity (earth and water). Oddly enough they also appear to correlate with the movements of the planets in the heavens—an observation which would undoubtedly have tickled Pythagoras pink!

There are a number of personality tests or inventories being used in contemporary psychological research. A number of these have been used in an attempt to assess whether or not there is a correlation between celestial events at the time of birth, as portrayed in the so-called 'astrological horoscope' (c.f. Appendix), and personality as assessed by such tests. Usually these studies have given negative or inconclusive results. Hume and Goldstein, for example, found no correlation between astrological data and personality as assessed by the HMPI and Leary system of Personality Diagnoses methods.[20] Now similar studies have been carried out which have been claimed to be neither inconclusive nor negative.

One of the most successful and widely used personality inventories is the Eysenck Personality Inventory (E.P.I.) developed by Professor H. Eysenck. The rationale behind this particular inventory is that people show physiological differences which divide them into dimensions of certain 'dispositions to respond'. One dimension is *In*troversion/*Ex*-traversion, the other *N*euroticism. The opposite dimensions are emotional stability and emotional instability. By analysing the results of a comprehensive questionnaire, the psychologist can apparently classify an individual into one of these categories with some success. Probably more important than the underlying rationale behind the E.P.I. is the fact that it gives reproducible and consistent results when used by various workers—a highly important quality for a tool used in psychological research. Using the E.P.I. alone and in a modified form the 'planets' and personality have expressed common interest.

A study was carried out by Eysenck and others in 1979 on over 2,000 adult subjects. The E.P.I. was administered and the subjects were assessed for extraversion and introversion. It was reported that, as predicted by astrological tradition, persons born under the *positive* Signs of the Zodiac showed a significant increase in extraversion over the average. Those born under the *negative* Signs were reported as showing a significant decrease, or introversion.[24]

Subjects were also assessed in his study to ascertain whether (as astrological tradition would maintain) people born under the water signs (Cancer, Scorpio, Pisces) were more emotional than those born under fire, earth or air signs. Again this was reported to be the case with a high degree of significance.

Gauquelin and others carried out a study on the personality dimensions of serveral thousand eminent European subjects, relating to the position of the planets Mars, Jupiter and Saturn at their times of birth. As well as assessing extraversion and neuroticism (and their opposites), the added dimension of psychoticism was assessed.[19]

A statistically significant correlation was found between planetary positions and extraversion/introversion and also psychoticism/non-psychoticism. In general the results again allegedly agreed with astrological tradition. For example, significantly more introverts were found to have been born when Saturn was either rising over the horizon or directly overhead at their time of birth. The extraverts were born when Mars or Jupiter occupied these positions. An interesting point mentioned in this study is that the highest significant correlation found between psychoticism and planetary positions at time of birth was in a group of Nazi leaders, and this correlation seems to hold for military men in general.

This observation is perhaps significant in the context of the correlation between profession and planetary positions established by Gauquelin and referred to earlier in this chapter. Thus the planets may correlate primarily with personality type, which in turn correlates with subsequent choice of profession, other things being equal. This is certainly a more attractive hypothesis than that which assumes a blind, impersonal correlation between natal planetary positions and subsequent choice of profession.

Despite the subsequent qualifications which have been applied to the first study on personality*, this second one remains unqualified, tantalizingly telling us that there is a scientifically validated, statistically significant correlation

---

*The first study referred to was published under the co-authorship of Mayo, White and Eysenck. It was presented at a conference in London in May, 1979. This conference was held at the Institute of Psychiatry in King's College Hospital where Eysenck is professor of Psychology. Not surprisingly, he gave a paper. In this he, not unconvincingly, tended to dismiss the findings which he had previously taken some pains to have published. In direct contradiction to what he co-authored in his published paper, 'Artifacts are unlikely to have produced the results obtained', he indicated that prior knowledge of astrology among the subjects tested probably accounted for the results obtained. This was despite the fact that he had effectively dismissed this precise proposal in the published paper. Prior knowledge of astrology could, of course, account for the results obtained. However, a more comprehensive analysis of these data by Mayo convincingly redressed the balance and implied that significant relationships—though not necessarily those published—did exist. At present we await publication of follow-up studies to confirm or deny these 'findings'.

At the time of going to press a separate group has apparently repeated Eysenck's findings with 'prior knolwedge' of astrology on behalf of its subjects being excluded.

between the position of the planets at our time of birth and objective assessments of our personality made much later in life. Indeed the results of other work not yet published by Gauquelin and a more comprehensive analysis of the initial personality study by Mayo confirm this thesis.

Such a concept is not so preposterous—as we shall see presently. The E.P.I. used in these studies is based, don't forget, on 'physiological difference' between people which lead to 'dispositions to respond': and 'physiological differences' leading to an increased tendency to respond neurotically, in an extraverted fashion or psychotically, may well be produced by planets. How? Perhaps in the same way as some of the other phenomena we have observed in this chapter which, as I have indicated, we shall pursue later.

The intention of this chapter has been to describe some of the evidence implying correlation between celestial events and events on Earth. Some of these correlations may just be coincidental, some may have quite simple and acceptable physical explanations, others may not. We shall now explore areas where we can see the boundaries of science extending to accommodate phenomena which at present we cannot explain simply or satisfactorily. These phenomena are no less incredible than correlations between planets, professions and personality types. Most of them, however, are more acceptable to conventional modes of thought.

CHAPTER III

Physics and Limericks

Current concepts in physics are quite simply incredible. They are so incredible in fact that in comparison an area of study such as astrology, which simply seeks to link celestial motion with human behaviour, seems a perfectly sensible realm of investigation. However, before attempting to assess the credibility or otherwise of alleged astrological phenomena it is important to consider both the relevance and scope of contemporary physics and also certain ideas which have been postulated concerning the nature and abilities of what we term 'mind'.

In this chapter I deal with contemporary physics on a general level and I would refer readers who required further elucidation of any points or subtleties to the Bibliography.

I have used limericks from various sources to illustrate some of the points I make in this chapter, simply because I like limericks. Where I don't reference a quotation or statement please relaize that

Anon. Idem. Ibid. and Trad.
Wrote much that is morally bad:

Some ballads, some chanties,
  All poems on panties—
And limericks, too, one must add.

We have already referred to Descartes in the context of his
belief that the pincal was the seat of the soul. His philosophy
and mathematics, of course, had a significant impact on
Western thought. One major aspect of this Cartesian philosophy is the 'principle of duality' which avers that the universe
is composed of two things—mind and matter: that thoughts
and things are complementary to one another in that they are
distinct manifestations of an underlying principle. To Descartes this principle would have been God. Mind, unlike matter,
cannot be 'touched', though it can be experienced. Most of
us would accept that the *intangible* mind is in some way linked to, or a manifestation of, the *tangible* and complex neurological circuitary of the brain. To say that the physical state
of the brain is affected by a particular state of mind and vice
versa would seem to be a reasonable assumption. To those
who accepted the Cartesian philosophy the presumption of
this 'principle of duality' was unquestionable. Today, three
centuries later, it is not possible to draw such a definite
conclusion. When seeking to study mind and matter we have
many other things to take into consideration. Odd things.

Many of us were bombarded at school with the notion of
protons, electrons and neutrons, nowadays we have to contend
with such creatures as muons and kaons, not to mention cas-
cades, omegas, pions and the ubiquitous quarks! These creatures are sub-atomic particles they are our contemporary
wanderers in the sub-atomic realm and are not the type of
thing we would normally associate with. They are of a different social class and live in a different and very eclectic
environment. They do however have strange behavioural
patterns which have special significance for us 'up here'.

It would appear that we live in a physical universe composed of particles which do not exist in space and time as
we understand it. Indeed, this physical world is utterly and
fundamentally insubstantial—just how insubstantial is indicated in the following quote from J. R. Oppenheimer: 'If we ask

55

. . . whether the position of the electron remains the same, we must say "No"; if we ask whether the electron's position changes with time, we must say "No"; if we ask whether it is in motion we must say "No".'[14]

The bewildering nature of our new-found sub-atomic entities is best exemplified by the particle called the neutrino. It has no mass, no field, no charge . . . nothing. It merely becomes conspicuous when it collides 'head on' with another particle. The neutrino also has an antiparticle (the antineutrino) which has exactly the same negative qualities! Having no mass, the neutrino can possibly move faster than light and hence, according to Relativity theory (which we shall discuss later) it can also move backwards in time as we know it.[4] The antineutrino, presumably, moves forwards! The novelist John Updike wrote a poem about the neutrino. I can't resist the temptation to plagiarize its concepts and transmute them into a limerick:

> Though neutrinos have charm and are small
> They arouse the pure physicist's gall—
> For their strangeness is such
> That they don't tell us much;
> They've no charge, mass, nor stature at all!

Such particles are the stuff of the universe as far as we can establish (or *our* stuff of *our* universe might be more accurate), even though they could well be mistaken for the products of science fiction. To look briefly at their world stretches our reason to its extremity and our credibility even further. Nevertheless the qualities possessed and expressed by these particles represent the structure, or potential structure, of our experiencable world within certain physical limitations.

One of the most singular and instructive features of the sub-atomic world is, paradoxically, its regularity. The physical quantities which define its particles are restricted to integral multiples of the basic unit by which the quantity is measured. Irrespective of the size of a particle, for example, its charge (unless it is uncharged) will be exactly equal or opposite to that of the electron, or exactly twice this. An arrangement

reminiscent of Pythagoras and his integral musical scales.[+]
The same principle applies to other physical quantities; hence,
for some reason, Nature at this level deals in round figures.

Equally singular and instructive is the fact that when particles are 'broken up' by collision with one another, they do
not produce constituent fragments of the original particles
but new particles, distinct, complete and independent. When
such a collision occurs it's as if a Mercedes Benz had collided
with a Rolls Royce, and out of the resulting chaos had emerged a Ford, a Volkswagan, a Honda motorcycle, and a bicycle! In other words, sub-atomic particles do not dissolve into
component parts, but transform themselves by interaction,
exchange of energy, and dynamic transfer of physical properties.

In a sense sub-atomic particles can be seen as the manifestations of a *materia prima,* a basic stuff of the universe which is
expressed by the dancing, weaving and transmutation of these
sub-atomic sprites. So what is this *materia prima,* what are
the elementary building blocks of matter, the neo-atoms as
it were? It is postulated that a distinct sub-atomic building
unit does exist. It is termed the 'quark'.

Apparently a number of quarks have to exist to justify their
existence, and they must have quite specific properties if they
are successfully to carry out their theoretical function of con-
stituting other particles! If quarks are taken too seriously in
actual physical terms, however, it appears that they present
the physicist with some severe theoretical problems. Nonetheless, the quark concept has led us some way towards being
able to describe the ultimate structure of matter. Molecules
composed of atoms, atoms of electrons and nuclei; nuclei of
hadrons*, and hadrons of quarks. S. L. Glashow, one of the
peers of the 'charmonium' or 'charm' (the proposed fourth
type of quark), has succinctly made the point that we seem
to be nearing the physical ultimate. 'Perhaps the impossibility

---

+Discussed in Chapter V.

*Hadrons are the particles which constitute the atomic nucleus, e.g.
proton, neutron, cascade, sigma, omega etc.

of *finding* quarks is Nature's way of letting us know we have reached the end of the line.'[7] For, despite an intensive 'hunting of the quark', it has not yet been observed. Molecules have been looked at, atoms even recorded on motion film, and sub-atomic particles made to dance before the physicists' instruments and eyes daily. The quark, however, is as yet elusive.

In 1931 the eminent physicist Paul Dirac suggested that space was filled with an ocean of electrons with negative mass and negative energy; he predicted that when cosmic bubbles formed in this ocean, positive electrons would also be formed. Whether or not there is a sea of negative energy surrounding us with bubbles and stretching positive holes is irrelevant, because the particles Dirac predicted should exist on the basis of this model surfaced one year after publication of his theory. They were called 'anti-electrons' or 'positrons'.

R. P. Feynman in 1949 proposed that positrons were not negatively charged electrons, but electrons travelling backwards in time. This concept is consistent with the Relativistic approach which we shall discuss imminently. Apparently Nature has no preferred direction in which time should flow. This proposal also gives an alternative explanation for the existence of antiparticles in general. Most sub-atomic particles have antiparticles, including (apparently) quarks. (Exceptions to this rule for some reason appear to be photons and eta particles.)

The realization of the existence of antiparticles gave rise to a new polarized God for the theoretical physicist, a new source of inspiration for the science fictionalist, and an ominous fear for the informed pessimist—antimatter.

Most physicists have recognized for some time the obvious fact that if antiparticles get together in the same relationship as non-antiparticles, then a piece of antimatter will result, i.e. a piece of matter effectively indistinguishable from its non-antimatter counterpart, but whose sub-atomic constituents carry opposite charges to those of the counterpart. Hydrogen atoms, for example, contain a proton and an electron, so if we mix an antiproton and anti-electron (positron) the result will be an anti-hydrogen atom which will show the expected properties of hydrogen. However, bring the two (apparently similar) atoms into close proximity and the resultant puff of energy will cloud the error of your ways.

To all intents and purposes antimatter at the gross level should behave physically and chemically in a similar manner to the matter with which we are familiar. Apparently a few discreet physical differences should theoretically exist between the two types, but that's all. We have referred elsewhere to the Tunguska meteorite which caused devastation in Siberia in 1908. It has been postulated that this was an antimeteorite, one composed of antimatter which, on meeting its complementary matter here, devastatingly dissolved into pure energy and havoc. True or not, we can be reassured that any bits of

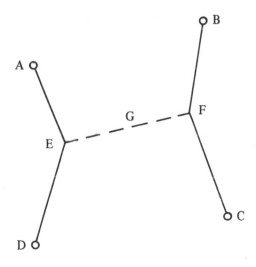

Figure 12: Sub-atomic particle collisions.

This diagram can be considered as showing particles A & D colliding at point E transferring energy along G and producing particles B & C.

Alternatively it can be considered to demonstrate the opposite. Collision of B and C at F forming A & D, in which case time flows in the opposite direction. Nature shows no preference for either sequence.

antimatter which reach the Earth's atmosphre should be small enough to disintegrate before touch-down.

Intriguing as they are in their own right, the most facinating aspect of the concepts (and actualities) of antiparticles and antimatter is the one initially put forward by Feynman with respect to the anti-electron: that these antiparticles are possibly running backwards in time.[2]

The mathematical interpretation of an anti-electron being a positron moving forward in time, or being an electron moving backwards in time, is absolutely identical. A particle moving from the future to the past is mathematically the same thing as an antiparticle moving from the past to the future. Intrinsically one postulate has no more credibility than the other, and we must accept the possibility that time to us is not what it seems to be and that either of these postulates is potentially valid. The cause of this state of affairs, of course, lies with Prof. Einstein and the fact that Nature's genetic shuffling occasionally produces the aces we term 'genius'.

Einstein published his special theory of relativity in 1905 and his general theory in 1915. The consequences of these theories were and are incredible, as we shall see.

In the relativistic universe all measurements of space and time are relative to the person measuring them; thus there is no such thing as an absolute space nor an absolute time. Any measurement of space or time has no *absolute* significance, it is only relative. What I would consider to be a specific time and place for a given event might be considered otherwise for someone who observes it from a different point of reference (or reference frame).

To illustrate this, suppose I had a twin brother sitting on the Sun, looking at his watch. Suddenly the Sun 'goes out'. He checks the time, (the watch being luminous!) and records it as 1 p.m. In his diary he notes, 'everything around me went dark at 1 p.m.'. As it takes around ten minutes for the light from the Sun to reach me here on Earth, I would notice the event as having occurred at 1:10. So my diary (written under electric light) would read, 'Sun went out at 1:10 p.m.' I would then await my twin's return to discuss this singular occurence.

When we met we would disagree about the time and the place. He would correctly state that the Sun went out at 1 p.m. immediately around him, and I would correctly state that it happened at 1:10 p.m. 93 million miles away from me. We would both be correct in a relative sense; neither of us would or could be correct absolutely.

Relativity demonstrates that simultaneity is a relative concept and that 'space and time'* are only descriptors, words we use to describe our observed environment. In fact, space and time are inextricably mixed together in what is termed the space-time continuum. Space-time, it seems, is some sort of universal fabric which can be wrinkled and crumpled at points particularly by massive objects such as planets, stars and galaxies which exert strong gravitational pulls on it.

The force of gravitation bends space-time locally and, consequently, at different points in the universe time runs at different rates. Time flow varies therefore with space-time curvature, and perhaps the most striking example of this curvature is illustrated by Black Holes. It is postulated that the following sequence of events leads to the formation of one of these astronomical wonders.

First of all, a star collapses in on itself due to the gravitational pull between its constituent particles. As this process continues, gravitational forces become immensely powerful and cause a massive curvature in 'local' space and space-time. Finally the force of gravity is so great, and space-time so curved in that area, nothing can escape and no 'signal' such as light can emerge from that region. The stage termed the 'event horizon' has been reached. To the observer no light can escape from the Black Hole thus formed, and time has stopped flowing.

---

*Note how the concept of space-time is incorporated into our language. We wait a 'long time' or a 'short time': we live a certain 'span' of years. We love 'always' not 'all time'. In an article in *Nature*, J. Gribbin informs us that a Chinese term for the universe is *yu-chou;* 'yu' means 'all space', 'chou' means 'all time'. He quotes this from a text of 120 B.C. He also informs us that as early as 300 B.C. it was taught that 'movement in space requires duration' (8) Shades of Einstein.

Despite the fact that light cannot emerge from a Black Hole, the fascinating observation has been made that Black Holes appear to emit certain particles at a steady rate. The potential significance of this observation has been described by S.W. Hawking in an article in *Scientific American:*

> One way to understand the emission is as follows. Quantum mechanics implies that the whole of space is filled with pairs of 'virtual' particles and antiparticles that are constantly materializing in pairs, separating and then coming together again and annihilating each other . . . Now, in the presence of a black hole one member of a pair of virtual particles may fall into the hole, leaving the other member without a partner with which to annihilate. The forsaken particle or antiparticle may fall into the black hole after its partner, but it may also escape to infinity, where it appears to be radiation emitted by the black hole.
>
> Another way of looking at the process is to regard the member of the pair of particles that falls into the black hole—the antiparticle, say—as being really a particle that is travelling backward in time. Thus the antiparticle falling into the black hole can be regarded as a particle coming out of the black hole but travelling backward in time. When the particle reaches the point at which the particle-antiparticle pair originally materialized, it is scattered by the gravitational field so that it travels forward in time.
>
> The emitted particles tunnel out of the black hole from a region of which an external observer has no knowledge other than its mass, angular momentum and electric charge. This means that all combinations or configurations of emitted particles that have the same energy, angular momentum and electric charge are equally probable. Indeed, it is possible that the black hole could emit a television set or the works of Proust in 10 leather-bound volumes, but the number of configurations of particles that correspond to these exotic possibilities is vanishingly small . . . Since the particles emitted by a black hole come from a region of which the observer has very limited knowledge, he cannot definitely predict the position or the velocity of a particle or any combination of the two; all he can predict is the probabilities that certain particles will be emitted. It therefore seems that Einstein was doubly wrong when he said, 'God does not play dice'. Consideration of particle emission from black holes would seem to suggest that God not only plays dice but also sometimes throws them where they cannot be seen.[9]

As space-time curvature depends on gravity and gravity depends on matter, and as matter by special relativity theory is really just energy, we find we live in a universe which is surprisingly neat and, at an intellectual level at least, relatively homogeneous in its fabric. Waves of energy, waves of matter.

By integrating Relativity and the sub-atomic theories, we obtain our most sophisticated theory of the physical universe which attempts to unify the microcosm and the macrocosm: the Quantum Field Theory. This informs us that there is a 'quantum field' which fills the universe, that this is the fundamental physical entity and that matter and hence space-time bending and so on are really just localized areas of intense field concentration. Matter forms field, field forms matter.

So matter and energy and space and time and the void and the manifest and you and I are one vast unified complex. The universe is a field from which everything emerges and returns. According to Einstein, 'the Field is the only reality'.

And this field is unified. What happens in one part of it affects what happens elsewhere. This is best illustrated in what is termed Mach's Principle, after its proponent Ernst Mach. According to this, the fact that material bodies resist being accelerated, i.e. demonstrate inertia, is not due to some intrinsic property, but is due to effects on them from other matter in the universe. Consider the case of a pendulum suspended by a thread so that it can swing freely.* If the pendulum is pushed, it not only swings back and forth in conformity with Newton's First Law of Motion, but gradually oscillates in a circular plane too, completing its circuit in twenty-four hours. As all motion is relative, we can glibly state that the Earth is at rest and the rotation of the pendulum was due to the rotation of the fixed stars around the Earth. These exerted an effect on it which caused it to oscillate in a circular plane. No one knows how the rotation of the stars

---

*The observations on the pendulum were first demonstrated by Foucault in the Paris Exhibition of 1851. The consequences of Mach's Principle in relation to physical phenomena such as inertia, the flattening of the Earth's poles and other areas is fascinating. The interested reader is referred to any good popular physics text to elaborate on the simple, if not simplistic, account given above.

does this. Commenting on this mystery Bertrand Russell said that although it 'is formally correct . . . the influence attributed to the fixed stars savours of astrology and is scientifically incredible'.

It is likely that *all* of our day-to-day physical laws are determined by the enveloping universe, both at the macroscopic and microscopic levels, to the extent that 'all our ideas of space and geometry would become entirely invalid if the distant parts of the universe were taken away'. This quotation is from Professor F. Hoyle who, perhaps ironically, indicated that an effect of planets on human development and behaviour was an absurd postulate.[10] It has also been stated that at the atomic level 'the objective world in space and time no longer exists'.[12]

Instead of taking bits of the universe away, however, let us look at a few more of its properties in the intact state. In particular let us look at some of the facts of relativity and space-time, that mysterious fabric where—unlike our expectations from our individually observed universes—'everything which for each of us constitutes the past the present and the future is given *en bloc* . . .' (de Broglie).[1]

From relativity theory we know that, as an object approaches the speed of light, mass increases, length decreases and time stretches relative to the observer. At the speed of light, mass is infinite, length non-existent and time infinite. This has been stated clearly through individual experience:

> There was a young lady named Bright
>   Whose speed was far faster than light:
> She went out one day,
>   In a relative way,
> And returned the previous night.

> To her friends said the Bright one in chatter,
>   'I have learned something new about matter:
> My speed was so great,
>   Much increased was my weight,
> Yet I failed to become any fatter!'   (Buller)

These facts are obviously not evident in our everyday world, but they are very much so at the sub-atomic level. This is simply because things in *our* everyday world do not move very quickly and, even at half the speed of light (1.5×10^5 Km per second), time only slows down 13 per cent. At the sub-atomic level things move quickly and hence these effects appear.

A particle moving at close to the speed of light, for example, will have infinite mass relative to its rest mass (i.e. its mass when it is at rest). If at rest it is spherical, it will be seen to contract into a flat disc as it approaches this speed. This phenomenon is termed 'the Fitzgerald contraction':

> A fencing instructor named Fisk
> In duels was terribly brisk.
> So fast was his action
> The Fitzgerald contraction
> Foreshortened his foil to a disk.

So too, the life time* (or, more precisely, half-life) of particles moving at speeds approaching that of light is significantly longer than that of particles moving less recklessly. It might be stressed that here, as elsewhere, when we refer to properties of particles, we are speaking in averages, in statistical terms, and not of individual particles. This point is worth stressing as not only does it demonstrate the statistical nature of physics even at its most fundamental level, but it also emphasizes the fact that the individual *must* deviate from the norm, and by selectng a statistical 'unit' at random you have something which in itself is atypical—a point we shall come to in a different context later.

A neat illustration of the principles at works here is given in Figure 13. At a given velocity the 'life times' of the particles are distributed about a norm. In other words, they exist for a certain time as a given type of particle before transforming into something else. As the velocity of the particles is increas-

---

*The 'life time' of a sub-atomic particle is the time it exists before it transforms (either spontaneously or through collision with another particle) into other particles.

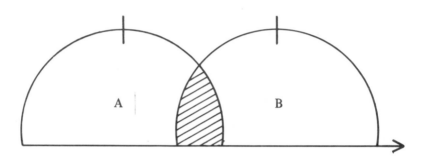

Figure 13: Half-life of sub-atomic particles.

A and B are curves representing the lifetime (half-life) of particles before spontaneous transformation. The velocity of the particles in curve B is greater than in curve A, hence time 'stretches' and they 'live longer'.

As this is a statistical phenomenon there is an area of overlap in 'lifetime' between the two groups of particles (hatched area).

ed they 'live longer and the norm shifts to the right'. Even so there is a degree of overlap and some particles moving with a slower velocity have a greater life span than similar particles moving with a greater velocity.

Again this elegantly and forcibly demonstrates the fact that physical laws are based on majority behaviour, on democratic principles. The exception is carried along in the generalization of statistical 'truth'.

As a further embarrassment to our reason we find that at the sub-atomic level when we study particle interactions, we discover that not only can particles apparently move backwards in time, but it is also quite possible that time can flow backwards too, and thus effect can also precede cause. If we remember the analogy used above, then the bicycle, the motorcycle, the Volkswagen and the Ford would all be formed *prior to* the collision between the Mercedes and Rolls which produces them. They anticipate their formation by existing and then the event which forms them occurs!

That these phenomena occur commonly in the realm of sub-atoms—the realm of the neutrino and quark, of fields and waves—indicates to us that our place in things must not be considered in exclusion. We too are lumps of matter, concentrated areas in the quantum field, intense, pulsing, cocktails of quarks, mesons, time reversal interactions and space-time warps. Our physical bodies cannot be taken in isolation, they *too* obey the enchanting laws which govern their constituents albeit in a, to us, less dramatic way.

It is when we come to consider what we mean by mind as opposed to body, however, that we find the same sort of paradox that our sub-atomic constituents meet microsecond after microsecond. Perhaps for this reason the problem of mind has attracted the physicist as much as the physiologist. Before we begin to approach the question of what we mean by mind, perhaps we should remember the lessons of relativity. It makes no sense to ask what is is a true length, a true time interval, a true sequence of events. It makes no sense to seek absolutes with ruler and clock. The time and space which we conceive is an interdependant, conceptually elusive thing, which can be distorted by thought as much as by gravitations. Its mystery is the charisma which draws us to it.

* * * * * * * * *

We entered the field of modern physics with reference to the Cartesian concept of duality. Mind distinct from matter. It would be presumptuous of me to attempt to 'stack the cards' on the side of either the dualist, *or* of the reductionist who would deny the independent existence of mind. I feel all that is necessary is to accept that there is some correlation between the physical organization of the brain and 'mind'. This correlate may well be an indirect one best illustrated by analogy.

If the neurology of the brain is represented by the circuitary of a television set, then mind can be represented by the signal which allows the circuitary to produce an image on the screen. (If you're materialistically predisposed, the signal can originate from the set itself and not from another, outside, source.) What I would tend to presume is that the screen *image* represented mood, a specific manifestation of mind, and hence by flicking channels, i.e. altering circuitary, a mood change could be effected as a consequence of a redirection of mind. (Having said this one accepts that many contemporary psychiatrists/psychologists accept the existence of only two moods, elation and depression, and conceive mind as a process, a dynamic state rather than a static entity.)

It is virtually impossible to discuss concepts such as mind without becoming enmeshed in epistemological niceties and, even if able to, I would feel this a waste of time in the context of this book, if not *per se*. I'd like to suggest two points in this context, however. Firstly, it seems unlikely that any entity—whether it be brain, mind or human being—can totally comprehend itself. If 'mind' reflects on the nature of 'mind', presumably something other than 'mind' must contain the objectivity necessary to reflect—a higher 'level of mind' perhaps . . . 'great fleas and little fleas'.* Secondly, as has been pointed out by many sages from Democritus to Erwin Schrodinger, all knowledge of the world *around* us rests totally on immediate sense perception, while on the other hand this knowledge does not reveal the relation of the sense perceptions to the outside world. To quote Schrodinger, 'In the picture or model we form of the outside world, guided by

---

*(For those unfamiliar with A. de Morgan's famous verse, here it is:

Great fleas have little fleas upon their backs to bite 'em,
    And little fleas have lesser fleas and so *ad infinitum*.
And great fleas themselves in turn, have greater fleas to go on,
    While these again have greater still, and greater still and so on)

our scientific discoveries, all sensual qualities are absent'.

In attempting to obtain knowledge we are bedevilled by the fact that sensory cognition and non-sensory cognitive processes are what really make our universe and we must accept the possibility that not only may we not be capable of knowing absolute truth, but that it may not exist. Truth too may well be relative:

> A monkey, a mouse and a mink
>> Were constructed in three ways to think;
> So the truth for each one
>> Differed slightly, and from
> The poor Dodo's whose truth is extinct.

So let's assume that there's no point in pursuing the nature of mind *directly*. What we can do, then, is to pursue it indirectly. By indirect methods we can often gain knowledge denied to us otherwise. The principle is best illustrated by the 'bugs on the sphere' analogy.

On a two-dimensional surface the sum of the angles of a triangle add up to 180°. On a three-dimensional surface this is no longer true. Suppose, therefore, that you were a philosophical bug and wanted to know if the surface you lived on was two or three-dimensional. You couldn't look at it, so how would you find out? Easy. Draw a triangle and measure the sum of its angles. If they add up to 180° you're on a 2D surface; if they add up to more than 180°, you're on a 3D surface. Fig 14. (If, however, they add up to *less* than 180°, then you shout 'eureka' and rush off to become an entomological Einstein.)

So what sort of triangles can we draw on our minds? We can, and do, anticipate and reflect, remember and feel. We can create images actively, or passively experience them in dreams. We can be conscious or unconscious and experience different states of consciousness in a continuum of awareness. We can alter mood at will or have it altered chemically or physically. We can, by hypnosis, remember in great detail things we have forgotten, or be told to do things we don't know we've been told to do until we've done them! We can

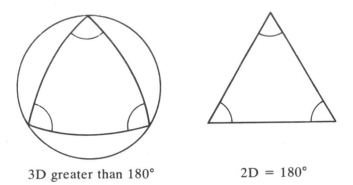

3D greater than 180°   2D = 180°

Figure 14: Angles of three-dimensional triangle.

hide childhood, if not neonatal and prenatal, traumas **and,** some would say, 'see' events in our minds either before **they** happen or when there is no'way of us experiencing them physically. We shall attempt to measure the angles of some of these mind triangles, but before this a word about knowledge.

Knowledge may be classified into four relatively distinct categories: empirical, rational, formal and intuitive.

Empirical knowledge is obtained by observation and experiment; it relies on sensory-cognitive processes and is the type of knowledge which constitutes science. Rational knowledge is the knowledge of reason and was the type mainly used in pre-scientific days. It should obviously be rational that time cannot flow backwards, that matter is not waves of energy and that particles with no obvious physical properties cannot have antiparticles. Rational knowledge has its source in our neurological reflections and also its limitations! Formal knowledge is powerful and puzzling. In a sense it is a composite of rational and empirical thought. It constitutes mathematics. For some reason mathematical truths exist awaiting to be discovered. They are abstract truths yet can produce tremendous tangible results. Formal knowledge is apparently 'in here' and 'out there'; it has, via a few symbols, given us the atom bomb. It is powerful and intriguing. Intuitive knowledge is the most neglected one. We 'know' things are going to occur, we 'feel' ominous portents of things happening or to come. Often they don't, but sometimes they do.

For the most part when considering the triangles of the mind we shall use the empirical, scientific approach. We must, however, be allowed the odd intuitive leap. One of the greatest advances in chemistry was the discovery of the cyclic structure of the benzene ring by Kekule; this discovery was not made empirically. Kekule dreamt that a snake was eating itself (Ouroboros in occult lore); on waking he transformed the cyclic snake structure into the benzene ring. What sort of knowledge was behind this discovery? Intuitive leaps often land on lush ground. A similar event happened to the Nobel prize-winning physiologist, Otto Loewi. It was directly through dreaming that he established the fact that nerve impulses are transmitted by chemical means.

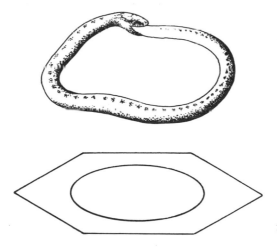

Figure 15: Kekule's dream.

It was by dreaming of a snake eating its tail (Ouroboros) that Kekule was able to envisage the structure of benzene as being cyclical.

At the outset let's assume that the world of mind and thought is enmeshed in the physical world as we call it. This is a useful model to use and we can accept a physical correlate or cause as we choose. The physical world is of the space-time continuum and the quantum field; it is composed of particles and is holistic. When considered in this context, we can draw correspondences as we like.

If I remember what I did yesterday, İ go back in time by changing my mental reference frame. However, the quality of my thought process is different, less distinct. Images of the past are dream-like. The electron becomes reflective, spins back in time and its quality is also different—it becomes a positron. An analogy between mind and particles.

Some physicists have attempted to actualize such analogies. V. A. Firsoff, for example, postualated the existence of elementary particles terms 'mindons'. These are somewhat reminiscent of Wilhelm Reich's 'orgons' or 'bions' in that they were presumed to constitute the 'mind-stuff'—if not, also, as the latter were proclaimed to do, the ubiquitous 'life force'. Like Reich and others, Firsoff suggested that mind was a 'universal entity', a postulate that might produce a knowing smile from a mystic.[5]

One of the most interesting theories hinting at the nature of mind which has been put forward in this context was the one postulated by Dobbs.[+] In this he postulates three spatial and two temporal dimensions. One of the time dimensions he postulates contains a 'ghost' of the future as it were. It is a dimension of 'objective probabilities' where the shapes of things to come weave their nebulous, but not yet definite, forms. Information about this probabilistic dimension comes to us in a stream of particles termed by Dobbs' psitrons'. These have physical attributes no more incredible than the psitron or neutrino. In essence the psitrons let us know how things are shaping up and presumably we can either let them do so or, knowingly or unknowingly, alter them. At one fell swoop precognition, determinism and free will take

---

+Discussed in detail in Koestler's *Roots of Coincidence* [12]

on a different texture. Dobbs' theory was evolved to account for precognitive experiences; however, despite its eyebrow-raising content, it strikes a chord of harmony somewhere.

Even to the most sceptical, the existence of precognition and extrasensory cognition (not *perception,* as this implies sensory involvement) should be accepted as a distinct possibility. I know few people who have studied the available literature and remained unconvinced.

The most intriguing offers of precognition are those given to us apparently during dreams. In 1927 J.W. Dunne published his book *An Experiment With Time.* In it he describes how, amidst the flotsam and jetsam of day-to-day dreams (or night-to-night ones!) there is a content which is definitely precognitive. This rather startling pronouncement has been confirmed by others in one way or another. In 1975 Krippner reported the results of twelve experimental dream studies involving telepathy.[13] Amongst other things he concluded that: 1. telepathy and dreams can be demonstrated in a laboratory setting; 2. the elements of orientation, expectancy and volition appear to be necessary for extrasensory effects to occur in dreams; 3. male subjects have been more effective as telepathic receivers in the dream experiments than female subjects; 4. telepathic effects have occurred in dream experiments when subject and agent have been separated by 60 feet, 14 miles, and 45 miles; 5. target stimulii that are emotional in nature appear to be more effective than non-emotional stimulii.

We have already mentioned the association between REM sleep and dreams. Virtually every mammal and bird studied demonstrates REM sleep.[6] Rosen in 1978 has demonstrated that the foetus, too, shows patterns resembling a crude form of wake, sleep and dreamlike states.[15] Does this mean that animals dream and that babies *in utero* reflect upon their imminent futures? Dunne quotes a case where a person dreamt about a situation which had a tragic outcome. When the dream actualized later, however, because of the foreknowledge it had given the tragic consequences were avoided.[3] This example gives strong hints of Dobbs' concept of a precast but potentially changeable future fed back to us occasionally by his psitrons. It also hints, as indeed do all precognitive experiences, at something in us which can move in a space-time continuum.

I don't want to pursue dreams to endless pages here, fascinating as they are, but I'd like to mention two further things about them. The first is an experience I had while trying to test Dunne's contention that some dreams are precognitive; the second, the possibility that we have recently found one of their physical causes or correlates in our brains.

For two or three nights I faithfully recorded key words about my dreams, on a note pad kept beside my bed, the moment I was alert enough to do so.

On one occasion I had written the following: 'Horses, Panama Canal, Peru, Pygmalion' and one or two other things. All I know about horses, by the way, is that they have four legs and you can tell their age by looking at their teeth. Nonetheless, I scrutinized the racing column of a newspaper next day—and surprise, surprise!

There was a race meeting on that day called the Panama Chase and a horse running in it called, not Pygmalion, but 'Pygalion' (or something similar). Not having the courage of my convictions, I didn't put money on it, which was just well as it came in last! On my way to work that same morning I passed the local library where a poster informed all and sundry that a lecture was to be given there about Peru. You can explain this however you will—that's what happened.

It is relevant to quote another personal experience here which I found very interesting, though it doesn't relate to dreams as such. I'd tried some image guessing tests one evening to see just how good I was as a 'sensitive'. Not surprisingly (to me) I was not much good. On one occasion out of perhaps twenty, however, I obtained the precise image my partner was projecting. My eyes were closed and on the black screen thus produced a silver shimmering daffodil drew itself in perfect form. I knew that was it—somehow things had come together and I was picking up someone else's projected image. I was correct.

To induce beautiful, if not precognitive, dreams you can smoke opium, the exudate from the unripe seed case of the poppy *Papaver somniferum.* Opium is a compound of opiates (morphine, codeine etc.), and recently, as we mentioned in Chapter I, opiates have been found in our brains. Although their pharmacology is at present being intensively studied, it is fascinating to reflect on what relation, if any, they bear to the handmaiden of sleep—the dream—and, if Dunne is correct, to precognitive phenomena.

Dreams, of course, follow sleep, and we have already seen how our brains contain the hormone vasotocin which is the most potent sleep-inducing substance known. Our heads, therefore, contain chemicals which could cause sleep and dreams—chemicals which correlate with the mind in the dream state, the state where its images often seem to emerge from a relativistic universe, one of distorted space and time.

I. W. Webster has postulated that 'with increasing age, events ordered in chronologic time produce a decreased awareness of the passage of time compared with that in a young person, i.e. time appears to pass more rapidly with age. For short-term processes, the converse would hold; time would appear to pass more rapidly in young persons . . . If time perception is disordered with age, this could explain some of the maladaptive phenomena of aging. Slowing of mental processes, perception, socialization and physical performance could be partly products of time relationships out of tune with the individual's previous norm and with the norms of other individuals and society.'[17]

Here again we see threads of relativity entwining with changes in physiological processes—hints that the function of the brain and of the mind will only be understood further in concert with our relativistic universe, and that the biological form of the brain determines how it communes with the universe.

* * * * * * * * *

Perhaps the most haunting of the sub-atomic sprites we have mentioned is the neutrino. Like a forgotten dream it is evident only by the effects it leaves. It is fitting, therefore, that the person who predicted the existence of this particle, twenty-five years before it was tracked down experimentally, was also instrumental in the development of a theory as intriguing to the rational mind as the neutrino. The person was Wolfgang Pauli, and it was through his collaboration with Jung that the latter developed his concepts of acausality and synchronicity. Perhaps, not without reason, the theory of synchronicity has been referred to by Arthur Koestler as 'perhaps the most radical departure from the world view of mechanistic science in our time'.

We have already seen the way space and time are inter-related and have drawn attention to the fact that comments on physical laws are based on statistical truths extracted from large numbers of measurable units, and not individual ones, as exemplified by particle physics. Jung's *Synchronicity:- an acausal connecting principle* uses these facts as premises and draws conclusions which enable us at least to have a framework for explaining phenomena such as precognisance which we might term 'coincidental', when it might not be.

Perhaps the most appropriate way of describing what the terms 'acausal' and 'synchronicity' mean is to quote them verbatim from Jung himself:

> ACAUSALITY. 'If natural law were an absolute truth, then of course there could not possibly be any processes that deviate from it. But since causality is a *statistical* truth, it holds good only on average and thus leaves room for *exceptions* which must somehow be experienceable, that is to say, real. I try to regard synchronistic events as acausal exceptions of this kind. They prove to be relatively independent of space and time; they relativize space and time in so far as space presents in principle no obstacle to their passage and the sequence of events in time is inverted, so that it looks as if an event which has not yet occurred were causing a perception in the present. But if space and time are relative, then causality too loses its validity, since the sequence of cause and effect is either relativised or abolished.'

SYNCHRONICITY. 'Despite my express warning I see that this concept has already been confused by the critics with *synchronism*. By synchronicity I mean the occurrence of a meaningful coincidence in time. It can take three forms:

(a) The coincidence of a certain psychic content with a corresponding objective process which is perceived to take place simultaneously.

(b) The coincidence of a subjective psychic state with a phantasm (dream or vision) which later turns out to be a more or less faithful reflection of a "synchronistic", objective event that took place more or less simultaneously, but at a distance.

(c) The same, except that the event perceived takes place in the future and is represented in the present only by a phantasm that corresponds to it.

Whereas in the first case an objective event coincides with a subjective content, the synchronicity in the other two cases can only be verified subsequently, though the synchronistic event as such is formed by the coincidence of a neutral psychic state with a phantasm (dream or vision).'

(From: Jung, C.G. *Synchronicity: an acausal connecting principle)*[11]

Now these definitions might seem a bit difficult to accept but let us not forget some of the facts which emerge from the relativistic and quantum-field universe. Acausality would, in a sense, be evident where time flowed backwards and effect preceded cause. Further, the three forms of meaningful coincidence are not only potentially explicable in terms of Dobb's theory of 'psitrons', for example, but are widely accepted as occurring. Most, if not all of us, have personally experienced (a) and (b), i.e. simple 'coincidence', and there is ample evidence to support at least the likely existence of (c).[3]

Jung's principle, valid or not, offers an explanation of 'meaningful coincidences'. It would contend that things which do not appear to be causally connected are related in a sense we might term 'symbolic'. Jungians take great pains to distinguish a symbol from a motive or sign. A trade mark, for example, is a sign and does no more than denote the object to which it is attached. A symbol, on the other hand, possesses connotations in addition to its obvious meaning. As well as denoting something evident, it implies something else, something which is often indescribable in language or rational thought. To most Christians Christ on the Cross has connotaion other than those of a man nailed to a piece of wood.

In a sense, the principle of the speed of light (i.e. the fact that its speed is constant irrespective of the movement of the source) is symbolic of space-time. We cannot directly experience a four-dimensional world, but the fact that we can measure something which connotes its existence tells us it is there in the same way that our triangle with angles that added up to more than 180° symbolizes a three-dimensional world.

Such symbolic features are characteristic of the very elegant system of Jungian psychology. In developing these concepts, Jung tackled a problem that, like relativity theory, should be self-evident but is not. The problem of chance. We glibly talk of chance and coincidence and the laws of averages, yet we do not yet understand what causes them. This would be relatively unimportant if it weren't for the fact that the whole of Western science relies on these 'laws', in the form of probability theory, on which to rest its case. What we do not understand is best illustrated by an example.

If we toss a coin once, we have an even chance of turning a head or tail. Indeed, if we toss a coin 10,000 times we shall more or less achieve 5,000 heads and 5,000 tails. This is a statistical truth. However, what is the situation when, as has been known, you toss a coin six, sixteen or twenty-six times and in each case turn up a head? Does the next throw have a fifty-fifty chance of being a head? Of course not. We can't keep getting heads; we *don't* keep getting heads. But why not? The coin still has a head and a tail and is unlikely to fall on its rim stand in place indecisively. What 'force' pulls it to the tail side after twenty-six or sixteen or six heads in sequence? I don't know, but such a 'force' exists and enables us to predict events in a statistical way as long as large numbers are used.[+]

But if we concern ourselves only with small numbers and obtain, for example, twenty-six heads in twenty-six conseccutive throws, what then? Such was the sort of problem Jung had tackled, arguing that if causality was only statistically true, then the exceptions, like a run of twenty-six heads, should have acausal explanations applied to them, and these explanations involved psychic contents interacting with external events.

And here again we arrive at a triangle of the mind containing more than 180⁰. *'Psychic contents interacting with external events.'*

H. Schmidt reported in *New Scientist* that by a subject 'concentrating' on a suitably prepared piece of equipment he could wilfully control the ostensibly random radioactive decay of Strontium 90. This experiment was statistically significant at the 0.001 level, i.e. the odds were 1000 to 1 against the effect being chance.[16]

For centuries we've struggled with the mind-matter problem, with the determinism free will problem and with the problem of objectivity and subjectivity. We classify knowledge, as I discussed, into different types, empirical, rational, formal and intuitive. Since the intellectual 'Renaissance' we have tended to accommodate empiricism, (with associated determinism, reductionism) and through necessity have accepted the ostensibly groundless but powerful tool of formal knowledge (e.g. mathematics). Other types of knowledge have all but been discarded. Yet what have we found? Time flowing backwards, Black Holes, neutrinos, antimatter, oceans of electrons with negative mass! In the presence of these, some of the discarded knowledge systems such as astrology seem eminently sensible. Jung stressed that individuals were 'small samples', that as such they cannot be carried off on the statistical tide. 'The only reality is the Field' and, as we are part of it, we are subject to its fluxes.

[+]'Probability' is further discussed in Chapter V.

Physics and Limericks

Koestler's praise for Jung's challenging ideas is certainly due. Concepts such as 'archetypes', the 'collective unconscious' and the one we have discussed, the theory of synchronicity, are indeed 'radical departures' from the mechanistic view. We say that sleep, and death, involve a 'withdrawing from the world around us'. This is untrue. Both of these in the relativistic universe are merely relative states of consciousness. In any observation, be it of galactic evolution or of processes of mind, there must always be something observing. The mind may reflect on itself, but any interpretation made of that reflection implies a distinct level of awareness. To the nihilist death brings nothingness. Must that too be perceived: if so, by what? These are questions for the philosopher or the mystic; being neither, I can leave them to others.

In this chapter we have seen the awesome concepts modern physics has brought to us: observed how some of the superior intellects of our time have penetrated again into the perennial problems armed with fresh weapons. Most of all, however, and this was the intention, we have seen that we cannot observe things in isolation. We are both part of and, at the same time, *are* the universe. It is in us and possibly outside us too.

We began with Descartes and the mind-matter problem as seen by him. I wonder if he were with us today what he'd think of this:

> There once was a wise man who knew
>   That his mind and his matter were two:
> 'Til his physicist son
>   Pointed out they were one;
> And his thoughts and his atoms were too.

CHAPTER IV

All that glisters...

In a world of myriad states of consciousness there seems to be one particular state which is unique and cross-cultural. It is temed 'the mystical experience'. To the Christian it is the experience of Divine love, to the Zen Buddhist—*sartori,* to the Hindu—*moksha:* and, although apparently without any particular preparation or expectancy it may happen to anyone, by all accounts a certain way of life is more conducive to producing it.

The aspiring mystic seeks 'illumination' by various techniques from the ascetic to the ostensibly indulgent. The end, however, would appear to be similar, if not the same, whatever the technique used: this is a state of tranquillity, inner calm and the certainty of something indefinable. A distinction might be made, however, between those who live a disciplined life in pursuit of enlightenment and those who don't but nonetheless actively or passively experience it, or something which hints of it. The unprepared person experiencing 'illumination' might not be expected to be permanently altered by the experience. Begging St. Paul's forgiveness, I would imagine that, for the most part, only those who train hard and long towards this specific end achieve maximal benefit from an experience of this type.

One might consider reported cases of 'ineffable union' by those whose only preparation was to swallow an hallucinogenic drug as being something less than instant mysticism. Hallucinogenic drugs, however, do produce states of enhanced awareness which may be akin to the mystical. Perhaps for this reason it has been advocated that the dying should, in appropriate circumstances, be given LSD.[5] This might not improve their expectations in this life but presumably could of the hereafter. Aldous Huxley, who elegantly described hallucinogenic experiences in *The Doors of Perception,* reportedly took an hallucinogenic drug on his deathbed. Presumably he felt it conferred some advantage when making one's exit.

Reported cases of mystical illumination in contemporary Western society would for the most part be regarded as being hallucinatory and possibly the consequence of mental illness. Recent clinical studies have proposed that the pineal gland might be the root of hallucinatory experiences.[7] These reinforce the observations made on animals in this context which were described in Chapter I.

It was also mentioned in the first chapter how metals were highly important in controlling pineal function. There was one group of people, of course, who also equated metals and 'illumination' and they did so often within an astrological framework . . . the alchemists.*

Until the eighteenth century there were only seven planets known (Fig. 16). Each of these planets had, and indeed still has, a distinct glyph or symbol to represent it. These symbols were not arbitrarily assigned, nor haphazardly arranged. The planetary glyphs form a symbolic path, one which was taken by the alchemists in their attempts to transmute what they termed 'lead' into what they termed 'gold'. To appreciate this symbolic path one must know that the original symbol for the planet Mars was ♂, a sort of bishop's orb. This is

---

*My discussion of alchemy is drawn from several sources. Two of the most readily available are given in the bibliography.[1][6]

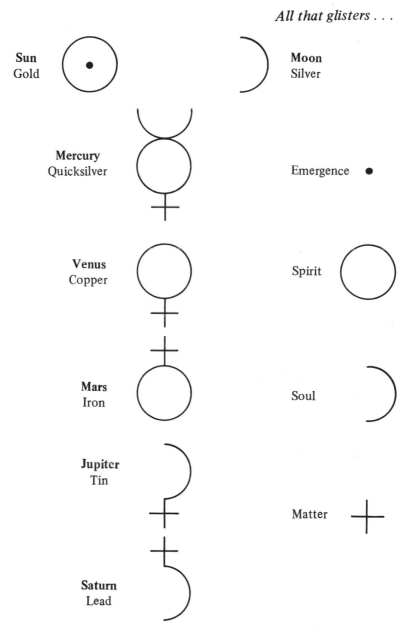

Figure 16: Planetary symbolism

written now as ♂ to prevent it being confused with Venus (♀).

Inspection of the symbols for the planets Sun to Saturn establishes that, with the exception of the Sun, they are composed of three parts only: a circle, a semi-cirlce and a cross. The Sun contains a central point which represents *emergence.* An understanding of this esoteric planetary symbolism should also give us an understanding of how the alchemist sought not necessarily only material gold, but spiritual gold, illumination.

Unlike the nuclear physicist, the serious alchemist was not solely preoccupied with turning one physical substance into another. Indeed, a cyclotron to an alchemist would have been like a psychotropic drug to a psychoanalyst: effective yes, but very subsidiary to the real end in view. Many of us think of alchemists as being bearded men with pointed hats covered in half-moons, transforming the base metal lead into the elevated metal gold. There are, of course, alchemical treatises in existence written in linguistic gibberish telling us precisely how to do this. Standing over a simmering crucible of vapourizing lead day after day is one of the most certain ways of driving yourself insane. One notable alchemist who, it has recently been claimed, ultimately suffered from lead poisoning was Sir Isaac Newton. The sensible alchemist would not do this, and consequently would not become insane and communicate gibberish. Yet he would still attempt to turn 'lead' into 'gold', at least according to the 'doctrine of correspondences'.

This doctrine is attributed to a gentleman of the pre-Christian era rejoicing in the name of Hermes Trismegistos ('Hermes the thrice great'). It is beautifully majestic in its simplicity and states that Man and the Universe are reflections of one another. What happens in the Universe (macrocosm) therefore is reflected in Man (microcosm) or, more succinctly, 'As above—so below'.

Man and the Universe accordingly are inextricably linked, and changes in one will result in changes in the other. Such a doctrine is at the basis of most occult arts. What the serious alchemist aspired to was mastery of the laws governing the correspondences between himself, metals and the rest of the Universe. He would then apply them towards his desired end.

To appreciate the viewpoint of the socially acceptable alchemist we must appreciate how this doctrine of correspondences integrated spiritual development, transformation of metals, and astrological, or more precisely planetary, symbolism.

If your refer to Figure 16 you will observe that each planet has a metal associated with it or, alternatively, each planet corresponds with a metal. According to alchemical philosophy cach planetary symbol also corresponds to a spiritual state in Man; so the arrangement of the three composite parts of the planetary symbol corresponds with a stage of spiritual development. Saturn, for example, has the cross of matter inhibiting the emergence of the soul (♄) and Saturn corresponds with the base metal lead. Hence when the alchemist spoke of transforming a base metal he was often being deliberately ambiguous. He could mean changing lead into something less base, or transforming himself so that his soul emerged from the cross of matter and opened itself to 'higher' influences. When the alchemist moved from the 'state' of Saturn to that of Jupiter, in alchemical terms lead became tin and in mystical terms he partially opened himself to some 'influence'. They all correspond: and note we again have this concept of 'opening' something in order, ultimately, to experience at a different level. Note, too, how these seven metals and planets can be made to correspond with the seven chakras described in Chapter I.

Now if you observe the planetary symbols you will see how the alchemist can, by transforming himself in a way which corresponds to these symbols, ultimately reach illumination or 'God'. By symbolically transforming lead into tin he has allowed the soul to emerge from matter and transcend it, Saturn becomes Jupiter and the man has the potential for further spiritual growth as his soul is now open and receptive. The receptive soul can now experience spirit, but only its stirrings. It is still sequestered in the physical body. The life force stirs; tin becomes iron, Jupiter becomes Mars—

the principle of life.

With the next transformation the spirit must emerge from the material chains: it must elevate itself from the restrictions of the body so that it is capable of being experienced in its proper realm. Iron becomes copper, Mars becomes Venus, the spirit emerges from matter though it remains linked to it. The final step looms. When copper is transformed into quicksilver (Venus into Mercury), then the alchemical work nears completion. The springs of a pantheistic God, His spirit Sun and Her soul Moon, can pour into the transformed soul of the alchemist and fill it with the ineffable: soul and spirit transcend matter. Then indeed lead has been transformed into gold, or base man has come to experience God. This God is androgynous, Father Sun and Mother Moon. The male and female aspects of the individual, the anima and animus in contemporary terms, has unified in a 'mystical' union or marriage.

Alchemists taught that before base metals could be transmuted into silver or gold they had first of all to be converted to their basic or fundamental nature or *materia prima.* If we jump to the spiritual correspondence here we are saying that, before being capable of experiencing God (gold and silver), the part of the base Man which can potentially experience God (soul) must be reduced to its fundamental form.

So what is the *materia prima* of soul? What is soul in its fundamental state? 'Unless ye be as little children ye cannot enter the Kingdom of Heaven', accords the Scriptures. Little children presumably have pure 'souls' having not had the opportunity to get up to much to defile them. Their souls are malleable, like metals. So when is the soul most unconditioned, most malleable, most fundamental? I would think the answer was obvious. At the time of birth. The soul, according to the alchemist, can be formed and transformed. If it forms in a way which makes it unreceptive to God, then it is base, and before it can work towards God it must be transformed.

Now if the soul is moulded from birth in the wrong direction spiritually, it has to be transformed or symbolically dissolved and recrystallized. One of the most potent agents for dissolving metals is oil of vitriol or concentrated sulphuric acid. The word 'vitriol' was much used by alchemists and is derived from the Latin for glass. Vitriol is also an acronym for *Visita Interiora Terrae Rectificando Invenies Occultum Lapidem* ('Visit the interior of the earth, through purification thou will find the hidden stone'). We could paraphrase this quite simply: 'Dissolve your base self, reflect and reform, and see clearly as through glass the hidden stone which is your soul in its most receptive state'.

So perhaps the alchemist sought to rediscover the receptive soul which he had at birth in order to transform its direction: and he did so by the symbolic and physical use of metals. Is there an inner and outer correspondence here too? Could metals *inside* the alchemist affect the receptivity of the soul, as, apparently, processing them outside could? Could the metals inside the body be instrumental in forming the 'soul'? The answer to this question is undoubtedly yes, and the planets themselves may well play their role in this, as we shall discuss shortly.

Despite what we have said, the alchemists were not just a bunch of chemistry-set mystics. They did apparently study chemistry, and particularly metallurgy, and made significant advances in knowledge in these areas. However, the true alchemist appreciated the esoteric significance behind his experimental ventures. Those who did not were referred to in a derogatory manner as 'charcoal burners'. They were the social group five of the alchemical world.

It seems, too, that the true alchemist could assess his progress along 'the path' by the physical manifestations which occurred in the metals he was handling. It is claimed, for example, that when the mystical marriage occurred in the alchemist he did indeed have the means *actually* to transmute lead into gold, and there are some intriguing accounts of such phenomena having taken place. However, these minor miracles do not concern us here. Let us simply consider alchemy as a symbolic path, through planets and metals, towards mystical revelation and see if we can make sense of it in contemporary terms. As a first step in doing this, let us take a closer look at metals.

A metal is a member of a class of substances characterized by specific physical properties. For example, metals are able to conduct heat and electricity well, to be deformed without shattering (they are malleable) and to be drawn out into wire (ductile). Metals are all crystalline in the solid state and exhibit a peculiar lustre. By adding other substances to pure metals, alloys can be formed which demonstrate physical properties quite distinct from those exhibited by the parent metal(s).

For millenia, metals have been utilized as a means of producing tools, jewellery, weapons, ornaments and so on. It is not surprising, therefore, that metallurgy is a very ancient science which was around long before the alchemists. As well as the obvious functions of metals in the solid form, in solution their salts form ions which show marked biological activity. This activity is not only restricted to the arena of normal biochemical function: metals are also used to treat illness.

In normal bodily processes metals perform a number of important functions. They are instrumental in carrying nerve impulses, enabling muscles to contract, allowing enzymes to function and performing a host of other processes necessary for life. It is quite evident therefore that any disturbance of the metallic environment of the body can have dramatic consequences for the individual.

A large number of metals is involved in bodily processes. It is relevant to note that 'the biological properties of the metals must be sought in the stability, stereochemistry and magnetic susceptibility of their complexes'.[3] In consequence any variation in these parameters would be expected to affect the metals' biological activity.

At one time or another all of the planetary metals were used therapeutically and two of them, iron and copper, serve important natural function in the body. Let's take a brief look at these metals which, for some unknown reason, were specifically chosen to relate to the planets of the solar system.

Gold of course is the most ductile and malleable of metals and with care gold leaf can be produced in which there are more than a quarter of a million sheets to the inch. Pure gold is very soft and yellow and is hardened by making alloys with copper and silver, thus producing gold of different purities. The purity of gold is measured in carats: 22 carat gold containing at least 916.6 parts pure gold per thousand, 18 carat 750 parts and so on, with pure gold being 24 carat.

One of the few solvents for pure gold is the mixture of nitric and hydrochloric acids called 'aqua regia'; however, gold is commercially extracted from quartz veins by amalgamation with mercury and from alluvial deposits by washing with water.

The main commercial uses of gold are in the manufacture of jewellery and coinage and in dentistry and gilding. In medicine gold therapy (chrysotherapy) is employed in the treatment of rheumatoid arthritis where gold salts are utilized. Gold foil is also applied to ulcerated skin to promote healing.

It is quite probable that gold exhibits an antibacterial action and that this accounts for its effects in rheumatoid arthritis where it suppresses or prevents the progress of the disease. Occasionally it produces dramatic remissions but overall, although alleviating symptoms, it doesn't seem to affect the outcome of the disease process.

Like gold, silver is also a precious metal with therapeutic properties. In the United Kingdom its purity is measured as Britannia Silver with 958.4 parts per thousand, or Sterling Silver with 925 parts per thousand. Its main uses are in the production of coinage and jewellery and, in salt form, in photography as it is light-sensitive.

In medicine silver has been used for centuries and indeed Paracelsus recommended its use for 'nervous disease'. As recently as the late nineteenth century 'Lunar caustic' (silver nitrate) was employed in the treatment of epilepsy. Silver is germicidal and its salts have local antiseptic actions. It is also a component of the powerful antibiotic silver sulphadiazine.

A singular feature of silver is the effect it produces when it is ingested in excessive amounts. Large quantities aggregate just beneath the skin and the portions of skin exposed to light, including the eyes, develop a bluish pigmentation. This condition is known as agyria. We accumulate quite a lot of silver in our bodies as we go through life, and when we finally reach the end we could, belatedly, be worth a bit in silver alone.

Perhaps the most paradoxical of metals, if not of all elements, is mercury. With a melting point of −39°C, it is liquid at normal temperatures. This bright, silver, dense, runny metal does indeed symbolize the qualities we ascribe to the word 'mercurial'. Quicksilver, too, is a beautifully descriptive word for it. The main use of mercury is in the chemical industry where it is used to form amalgams for the extraction of metals from ores.

Mercury salts and derivatives have been used in medicine in a number of areas. They have been used as antiseptics, preservatives, parasiticides and fungicides. Mercurials were amongst the first drugs successfully used to treat syphilis and they were potent diuretics (drugs which promote urine excretion). Because of their toxicity, however, and the development of alternatives, mercury-based drugs are now almost completely unused.

With copper we have one of the industrially ideal metals in terms of abundance and physical qualities. This reddish-brown element is hard, flexible, tenacious, ductile, malleable, and has good electrical conductivity. It is used, therefore, for a number of purposes including coinage and electrical wiring, and is alloyed with tin to form bronze and brass.

While copper salts have been used in medicine as fungicides and astringents and, as copper sulphate, has a very potent emetic, it is also the first of our 'planetary metals' which is essential for human metabolism. Copper deficiency results in blood disorders and bone disease. Copper is essential for the proper functioning of iron in the body, and indeed copper and iron metabolism seem inextricably linked. In the body there are relatively high concentrations of copper in the brain, implying that it plays an important role in its functions.

The second 'planetary metal' essential for human metabolism is iron, one of the oldest metals known to Man. The myriad uses of iron are well known and need not be detailed.

Iron, of course, demonstrates that very peculiar phenomenon—magnetism. Iron is very easily magnetized and most of us have seen it sprinkled on to sheets of paper held over a magnet to outline the shape of the magnetic field.

Although it is a very important substance in normal metabolic function, its only use in modern medicine is in the treatment of iron deficiency (anaemia). It is interesting to note how iron was empirically used to treat anaemia even many centuries ago. It was believed that it was imbued with the strength of the god Mars and patients who were weak and had a marked pallor were given drinking water in which old swords had been allowed to rust. Strength from Mars or iron from the water, either way it worked.

Because of the relative ease with which iron atoms can lose or gain electrons, iron plays some particularly crucial roles in body biochemistry including the production of the substance which stores the energy we use, adenosine triphosphate (ATP). Iron is an important co-factor in a number of enzymatic reactions, including those involved in melatonin synthesis as described in Chapter I.

Tin is a bright white metal in its pure form and it doesn't tarnish in air. It is fairly soft, ductile and malleable; at 228°C, however, it suddenly becomes quite brittle. It is a relatively poor conductor of electricity.

Depending on temperature, there are two types of elemental tin: white tin and grey tin. White tin has a density of 7.3 and is converted to grey tin (density 5.8) at temperatures below 18°C, and vice versa.

The main uses for tin are in the production of tin plate, bronze and tin foil. Tin sulphide, which is bright yellow, is used in gilding.

Tin salts are still used to treat boils, carbuncles and acne but are probably of little use in these respects.

The last of our 'planetary metals' is lead, the bluish-white substance of remarkable plasticity. From bullets to soundproofing and plumbing, lead has a great number of applications.

Lead today is *materia non grata* in medicine, despite the

fact that lead compounds used to be used extensively as astringents. Lead is very toxic and ingestion can cause mental retardation and chromosomal abnormalities. A number of cases of lead poisoning used to occur from whisky illegally brewed in lead vats. Moonshine would have been more appropriately named Saturnshine!

* * * * * * * * *

The intention of the alchemist with his metals was not always mercenary, many seeking to transform themselves spiritually— following the principle *'Solve et coagula'*. The imperfect soul was 'dissolved' to its *materia prima,* then 'recoagulated' into a purer form, this purer form occurring when the masculine and feminine or active and passive aspects of the personality became integrated.

To the alchemist the non-metal sulphur corresponded to the active in nature and the metal mercury to the passive. The mystical marriage, the formation of the androgyne, was produced by a unification of active and passive, male and female, spirit and soul, sulphur and mercury.

This correspondence is interesting because both sulphur and mercury are highly relevant to the planetary metals with respect to both their free-state occurrence and biological activity. Mercury itself naturally occurs as mercuric sulphide and has a very high affinity chemically for sulphur.

Iron, lead and copper occur quite abundantly as sulphides and tin, which occurs as the oxide, has sulphur associated with it in tinstone, the main source of the oxide. Silver has a great affinity for sulphur and becomes tarnished due to the formation of silver sulphide. Gold too can be linked to sulphur to form aurothic chemical groups which are biologically active.

Many of these metals are extracted by the process of amalgamation whereby their ores are 'dissolved' in mercury and then separated in purified form. Further, the biological activities of at least gold, silver, lead and mercury are almost certainly, and possibly exclusively, related to their abilities to combine with sulphur in the body.

Hence we, like the alchemist, can see that sulphur and mercury play a significant role in the chemistry of the planetary metals.

* * * * * * * * *

Like other atoms, metal atoms can lose or gain electrons and do so when they take part in chemical reactions. The tendency for a metal to do this can be measured and hence quantified and given a value. This is called 'the standard oxidation potential'. Metals which are not very active and which do not very easily give up electrons are termed *electronegative;* those which do release electrons easily and which are active are termed *electropositive.*

If we place the Earth in its appropriate place in the solar system, we find that it sits in between Mars and Venus. Thus stacked on one side of us are the Sun, Mercury and Venus and, on the other side, Mars, Jupiter and Saturn. Let us substitute the appropriate metals for these. Above us we have copper, quicksilver, silver and gold which are all electronegative, and below us iron, tin and lead which are all electropositive. Fig. 17*The earth-centred universe of the alchemist is polarized into positive and negative. It is chemically yin and yang.

Metals conduct heat and electricity, and their ability to do this can also be measured and expressed quantitatively. The units used to measure electrical conductance are termed 'specific resistivity'. The ability of metals to conduct heat or electricity is significantly altered when the metal is liquid hence quicksilver, which is liquid, is not directly comparable with the others in this context. We find, when we remove

*The moon also fits this pattern if it is placed, as it lies, nearer to Venus than Mars.

	Electronagative			Electropositive		
gold	mercury	copper	⊕ Earth	iron	tin	lead
⊙	☿	♀		♂	♃	♄
Sun	Mercury	Venus		Mars	Jupiter	Saturn

Metal
Standard oxidation potential (volts)

gold	(Au/Au^{3+})	-1.50	iron	(Fe/Fe^{3+})	+0.036
mercury	(Hg/Hg^{2+})	-0.789	tin	(Sn/Sn^{2+})	+0.136
copper	(Cu/Cu^{2+})	-0.337	lead	(Pb/Pb^{2+})	+0.126

Figure 17: The polarity of the earth-centred solar system.

errant Mercury from the planetary system, a singular fact. The *orbital motion of the planet correlates in sequence with its corresponding metal's conductivity.*[2] Let me explain further.

If you look at Table 3 you will see the planets, with the exception of Mercury, listed in order of mean orbital motion relative to the Earth. Notice how the speific resistivity or ability to conduct electricity of the corresponding metal correlates with the orbital motion. As the speed of the planet in its orbit decreases, the resistivity of the metal increases. (The same type of relation is true of the heat conductancy of these metals.) The slower a planet moves the less able its corresponding metal is to conduct electricity!

The correlation between electropositivity and electro-negativity and the planets' position relative to Earth may be spurious; so too may be the correlation betwen orbital speed and conductance of heat and electricity. Then again they may not be. Someone, sometime, associated specific planets with specific metals for some reason. The fact that these specific physical properties were apparently not known until recent times makes the relationship even more intriguing. Let's take the intrigue further still.

In Chapter II we considered some phenomena in which planetary movements corresponded to events on Earth as varied as susceptibility to polio and radio disturbances. Let us look at another such phenomenon—one of which I've had personal experience.

Most people have heard of Rudolf Steiner who founded the Anthroposophical Movement and who was active in progressive and remedial education.

As well as having novel and practical appraoches to education, Steiner's philosophy encompassed more esoteric subjects. These included planets and metals. Steiner apparently believed that in their solid states metals were unresponsive to planetary influences, but when in solution they would respond. So, too, like the alchemists, he considered certain metals corresponded to certain planets. Being a busy man, as well as a sensible one, he delegated the testing of this hypothesis to one of his pupils, Frau Kolisko.

Between 1928 and 1952 Kolisko performed many (relatively simplistic) experiments to test Steiner's idea that, when in solid form, metals were 'subject to the forces of the Earth but . . . when in solution the planetary forces come into play'. Let us remember at this juncture that in people metals are effectively 'in solution' and hence, if Steiner's postulate is correct, subject to 'planetary forces'.

Perhaps not surprisingly Kolisko and other followers of Steiner confirmed Steiner's beliefs in this respect. I will not give details of their findings as the interested reader can interpret them by reference to published works by Kolisko and another lady called Agnes Fyfe. Similar studies have, however, recently been repeated using more sophisticated methods.

When solutions containing silver are added to solutions containing iron, the iron displaces the silver from solution and causes it to precipitate. The precipitated silver becomes black on exposure to air. If a solution of silver and iron salts

TABLE 3

Planetary motion and physical parameters

Planet	Mean orbital motion (degrees per day)	Planetary metal	Electrical conductivity	Heat conductivity
Moon	13.2	Silver	1.47	1.002
Mercury[+]	1.4	Mercury[+]	94.1[+]	0.019
Venus	1.2	Copper	1.55	0.962
Sun	1.0	Gold	2.05	0.762
Mars	0.5	Iron	8.9	0.199
Jupiter	0.08	Tin	11.5	0.162
Saturn	0.03	Lead	19.2	0.086

+(Mercury is a liquid and therefore cannot be directly compared with the other planetary metals.) Note how, with this exception, as the mean orbital motion of the planet increases, so does the electrical conductance of the corresponding metal. The opposite applies for heat conductance.

is mixed in a dish and a cylinder of filter paper is placed in the dish, the solutions rise up the paper by capillary movement and the silver is precipitated out on to the paper. This produces 'forms' of silver on the paper and hence one can observe the precipitation occurring. (Fig. 18) Silver, remember, corresponds to the Moon, iron to Mars.

Every month as the Moon orbits the Sun it conjuncts Mars (0° aspect). In August, 1975, the above procedures were carried out and it was found that about fifteen minutes prior to the time of the exact conjunction, silver precipitated out

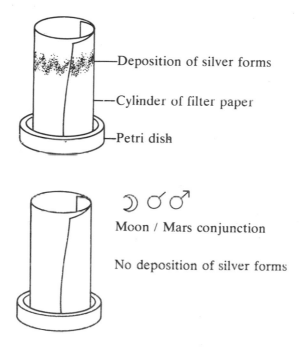

Figure 18: *The effects of planets on metals in solution.*

on the filter paper as normal. Four minutes before exactity of conjunction the silver seemed reluctant to be precipitated, and at the exact time of conjunction between the Moon and Mars (0614 *GMT*, 30th August) the silver did *not* precipitate out. About three-quarters of an hour later silver again began to be displaced by the iron.

The precipitation of silver by iron occurs quickly, but the reaction can be slowed down by the addition of lead. Lead, of course, corresponds with Saturn and so with mixtures of lead, silver and iron solutions it might seem sensible to look at Saturn, Mars, or Saturn-Moon-Mars effects on this reaction. In 1976 there was a Saturn-Mars conjunction (this occurs every two years): during this period the same procedure was followed, though now lead (nitrate) was added to the dish containing silver (nitrate) and iron (sulphate).

As before, prior to the Mars-Saturn conjunction silver was (25%) precipitated by the iron: a little lead moved into the filter paper also, though it should be stressed that lead should not chemically affect the iron-silver reaction. At the time of the Mars-Saturn conjunction, however, although the precipitation of silver was *not inhibited,* the appearance of the 'forms' was. Further, most (70%) of the lead moved into the filter paper. It took several days for the reactions to return to 'normal', i.e. the metals behaved and forms appeared 'normally' once the Mars-Saturn conjunction was completely over.[4]

These experiments were fairly well controlled and apparently conclusive. Planets seemingly affected the behaviour of metal ions in solution. Hints of alchemy. Like Thomas, I had to see for myself.

In June, 1978, Mars again conjuncted Saturn. I repeated the experiments myself and also carried out another series involving the metal manganese * in triplicate. Every day for about a month I set up filter papers, mixed solutions and ran controls religiously. Despite some suggestive findings, I did not get a conclusive result on the iron-silver-lead system.

I ran the manganese experiment because I was not convinced that even if the planetary effect existed it was indeed specific for certain metals only. Oddly enough, although the iron-silver-lead results were not particularly impressive, the rate of manganese reaction dramatically altered on the evening of the Mars-Saturn conjunction. Although controlled, this latter experiment was merely a preliminary run as far as I was concerned, and I am not yet convinced. I accept, however, that a number of people have obtained quite dramatic results in this area of study and that such effects occur. If it is accepted that such effects of relative planetary movements on ions in solution do exist, then the question 'how?' is a prickly one. With the known physical forces in nature it is

---

*Reduction of potassium permanganate by citric acid using lead sulphate and water as test and control solvents

difficult to explain how a planet such as Saturn, which is relatively small and very far away, could possibly affect ions in solution. However this is no reason for closing our eyes to the possibility of such effects which can be tested simply enough in any laboratory.

There is one final comment, faintly amusing, which I should make on my involvement in these studies. It is becoming progressively more accepted in scientific circles that an experiment is not simply a scientist studying an experimental system objectively. The tendency more and more is to see the scientist as *part* of that system, a participator as well as experimenter, and hence the results obtained are a product of the whole system including the experimenter (himself or herself). This concept has emerged most strongly in the field of sub-atomic physics, and higher up the physical scale the practising physician probably appreciates its validity more than most when he observes that drugs *plus* good bedside manner work best!

When I informed associates of mine well versed in astrology about my inconclusive results with lead and iron, they were quite unperturbed. They pointed out that when I had carried out the experiments my own birth chart had Saturn transiting Mars, exactly to the degree, i.e. Saturn in its orbit was passing exactly the same place Mars had occupied at my time of birth. That, they informed me, was why my results were inconclusive. Saturn and Mars, of course, do not familiarize with manganese. I don't know if the implication was: a fairly critical scientist, yes—but an uninformed alchemist!

* * * * * * * * *

We began this chapter by reference to mystical experience and we have moved some way on from that: let's return. William James eloquently informed us of the fact that there are many varieties of religious experience, yet, as we mentioned earlier, they do seem to have something in common. If you've had a mystical experience you know it. No description will do it justice or convey its essence to anyone else, but it is signularly informative to you and about you.

Now if such experiences are so similar in end product, presumably they might be expected to have similar physical correlates too. There are many varieties of sleep too, after all, and when we sleep most of us are lying down with closed eyes and probably secreting chemicals such as vasotocin into our brains. These are the physical correlates of sleep. What physical correlates might there be between us and the ineffable? For millenia the pineal has been considered something special in this respect. The Crown Chakra, the Seat of the Soul, what better than the third eye as a source of the physical correlate of enlightenment and illumination!

Highly speculative it may be, but I feel one could seek the physical centre of illumination in the pineal as tradition would allow. We have seen how the pineal appears to be inextricably linked in processes associated with hallucinatory experience and with the 'chemicals of the mind'. More importantly in this context it appears that when the pineal is stimulated in a human being the sensation of 'light' is experienced; how this has been done will be described in the next chapter. We see therefore (and we shall discuss this in greater detail in the final chapter) that the pineal seems to have strong associations with things ineffable which we experience. Sleep, dreams, hallucinations. The presumed realm where mystical illumination waits. But how does it get there?

As I implied before, I feel 'instant mysticism' is exceptional if not non-existent and that those who achieve 'illumination' are generally, if not exclusively, those who train for it as the alchemists did. How therefore do we link alchemy with the pineal and illumination? I don't know. However, there are some vague hints which may give us a whisper of something.

Like any other system of religious attainment or spiritual pursuit, alchemy was strictly formalized, routine, and to most of us would probably have been a most boring profession. Accounts of how the alchemical work was performed are littered with the word 'repetition'. Like repetition of mantras, prayers, use of prayer beads or yogic breathing the repetitive nature of the alchemist's work probably produced changes in him making him calmer and more receptive.

Such mood changes would be correlated with physical ones and there is no need to say where one feels these may have occurred. But what involvement, if any, would we expect the planets and metals to have in this process? Again one must be highly speculative.

The planetary symbols as we saw can be interpreted as the spiritual path taken by the alchemist: but could the planets have been more directly involved in the mystical union?

The experimental evidence which to date has been given asserts that planetary movements and specific planets affect metal ion activity. The metals ostensibly affected include iron, a major co-factor in the synthesis of melatonin by the pineal. If this indeed is the case, did the alchemist know this information—use it? (Remember Descartes' etching!)

Further, there are these intriguing relationships between planetary position and movement and contemporary electrical and electro-magnetic phenomena. As we shall discuss in Chapter VI, with respect to altering cellular function in tissues and organs, 'electricity works'. So we have a few hints and perhaps a slight whisper of something.

I do not intend to speculate any further on this, just to say one final thing. It is now technically possible to measure certain aspects of pineal activity in human subjects, including the amount of melatonin they produce. It would be interesting to compare a group of mystics or monastics with a control group of the less spiritually inclined in these terms. The hypothesis is speculative but testable: the mystic's 'mind' may produce something more, or less.

CHAPTER V

Number, sound and form

We have already met the movements of the eyes which correlate with dreaming, the so-called REMs. There are also LEMs or lateral eye movements.

For many years now it has been accepted by physiologists that in right-handed people the left hemisphere of the brain is 'dominant' and vice versa. The non-dominant hemisphere is termed 'minor' or quiet. The speech centre is almost always situated in the left hemisphere which, as most people are right-handed, is most commonly the dominant one. We should remember that the optic nerves which carry the light impulses from our eyes to our brains cross, so that the right eye feeds the left hemisphere and vice versa. Lateral Eye Movements tell us something about 'dominance' and 'quietness'.

When asked a question, people will often glance slightly to the right or to the left before answering. The direction of this initial gaze is thought to be an indication of hemispheric activity. Investigators have found that right LEMs (left hemisphere) are usually associated with verbal and sequential processes while left REMs (right hemisphere) are usually related to spatial tasks. Recent research has also linked the right hemisphere with emo-

tional processes. . . and there are indications that the right hemisphere may be involved in such things as creativity and intuition.
Meditation, hypnosis and drug use (alcohol, marijuana and
cocaine) have also been mentioned in association with right
hemisphere activity. It has been suggested, for instance, that
some types of drug use may be related to attempts to temporarily free the right hemisphere from the left's dominance in order
to produce states of consciousness associated with the right
hemisphere.

(Trotter, 1976)[16]

With the sophistication which has entered neurosurgery we
have been able directly to accumulate evidence about physiological functions of different parts of the brain. There is now
impressive evidence to suggest that the dominant hemisphere
is involved mainly in language ability and logical processes,
and the quiet hemisphere in spacial and intuitive processes.
These hemispheres have also been termed 'solar' and 'lunar'
respectively.

One of the pioneers in the use of brain surgery as a means
of assessing the anatomical and physiological correlates in
the brain is Dr. Wilder Penfield. No general anaesthesia is
required for brain surgery as the brain, once the scalp and
skull have been penetrated, has no nerves which cause sensations of pain. It is possible, therefore, to stimulate parts of
a patient's brain electrically during surgery and obtain a
verbal report on the patient's subjective response to that
stimulation. In this way, in concert with the known effects
of removing parts of the brain, a map can be drawn which
correlates physical parts of the brain with mental processes.
To all physiologists the most well-known map of this type
is Penfield's homunculus (Fig. 19), a well-known and well-
loved, albeit grotesque, individual. Penfield has observed that
after innumerable surgical procedures, often involving removal
of large segments of brain, the 'mind' seems in some way
to be independent of the brain; as he says: 'The machine
will never explain man, nor mechanisms the nature of the
spirit'.[11] A statement which presumably arose from his right
hemisphere, unless he is left-handed!

It might be mentioned that, included amongst the many

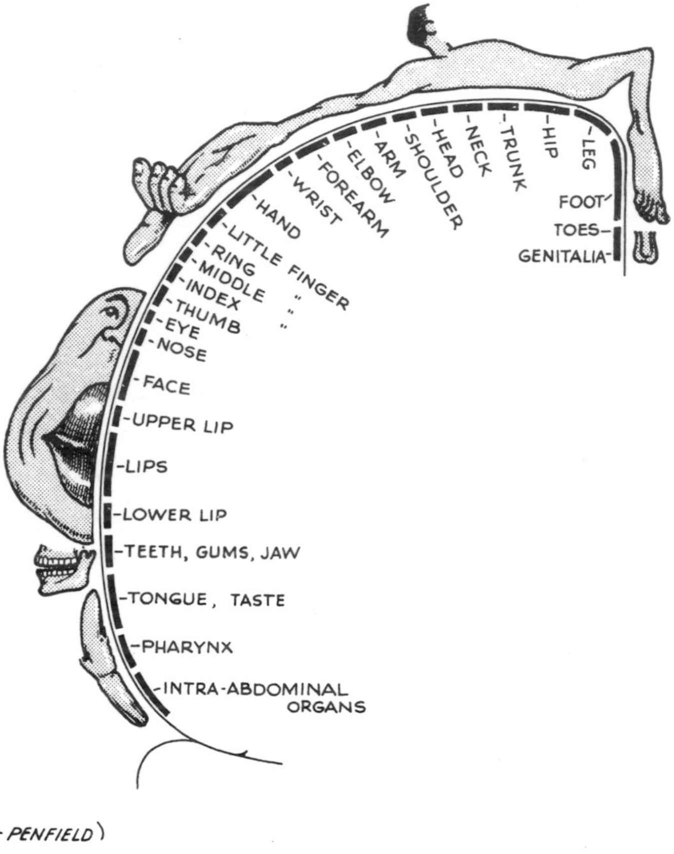

(After PENFIELD)

Figure 19: Penfield's homunculus.

Sensory homunculus. The size of each body part represents the proportion of the part of the brain which deals in sensory perception devoted to it. Thus the lips and tongue are highly sensual things, the wrist and little finger aren't!

(From W. Penfield & T. Rasmussen (1950), *The Cerebral Cortex of Man*, p. **44**. New York: Macmillan)[11]

things stimulated in conscious human subjects during brain surgery, has been the pineal gland. Apparently stimulation of this produced the subjective experience of 'light'.

So it seems that to a relative degree each hemisphere of

our brain deals with different inputs and outputs: the dominant with articulation, logical and rational thought; the quiet with intuition, creativity and aesthetic matters. Such as music.

The association between music and mood states is self-evident and all of us who are not deaf have directly experienced it. Science holds no brief for the self-evident however and music, like other self-evident things, has been duly investigated.

The electrical potential of the skin alters with mood and the galvanic skin response, or GSR, can be used to assess mental states. By monitoring this it has been demonstrated that music can reduce anxiety to such an extent that it has been termed an 'emotional scapegoat'.[12]

Music has been used successfully as an adjuvant in the treatment of mentally disturbed individuals. In 1976 Wilson,[19] for example, described how disruptive behaviour among young children could be suppressed by musical conditioning, and Smith[15] in 1975 stressed forcibly the importance of a high intensity of musical activity in work with young adult psychiatric patients. Music, however, is not *always* therapeutic.

It is common knowledge that music which has a high volume can cause damage to hearing in people constantly exposed to it. However, it is not only volume that can be unnerving about music, but also its composition. Ryan has described the sorry situation where up to seventy-five per cent of musicians playing in an orchestra have become unwell when playing modern works.[14] Apparently the discord in these works has produced discord amongst these musical martyrs, causing them to become nervous, irritable and tense, and to suffer from insomnia and even bowel disorders!

The relation between music and such things as nervous tension has been investigated in another way. Some years ago an article was published describing an experiment on music and mood. Basically the theme was as follows: a group of subjects were entertained by a piece of music and asked to note their subjective feelings about it. They all thought it very pleasant as it had been played well in the way the composer had intended it to be. The beat was perfect and everyone was happy. Then the subjects were divided into two groups and one group was given a tranquilliser, the other a placebo[+] as a control. They were then entertained again but the piece was played slightly jarringly out of rhythm. To no one's surprise the tranquillized group observed no difference in the music, but the control group showed distinct signs of disturbance of a mental, if not gastrointestinal, nature.

Such effects of music are to be expected. Its beat and rhythm would appear to be linked to us in some mysterious way which may well equate with the beats and rhythms of our bodies. Apparently if a sound is played with the same frequency as your heart-beat, and then made to beat slightly out of phase, that is also disturbing.

Sound has three characteristic properties—pitch, volume and quality. Sound is produced by vibration and the frequency of vibration will determine whether the sound produced is high or low, i.e. *frequency* of vibration will determine pitch. Strength or amplitude of vibration, on the other hand, will determine the volume of a sound, more intensive vibration producing louder sound and vice versa. The most intriguing feature of sound, however, is its quality or timbre.

Different things vibrating, be they voices, instruments or electric drills, can produce the same note. It will sound in some way different to us however and will have different 'quality' There is obviously a different quality of sound between my whistling a Beethoven piano sonata in my bath and Rubinstein playing the real thing; but why? Overtones. Along with the basic or fundamental note being played are a number of other ones—sequestered yes, but still present. The variation in intensity of these overtones, or harmonics, determines the quality of the sound. We shall return to overtones later in another context and shall then refer to them by their synonym 'harmonics'. The term 'colour' is also applied in this context to notes from different sources, and a spirited attempt has been made to *actualize* this term musically.

+An inert but not necessarily inactive substance.

W. Garner attempted to link music and colour directly and suggested that the 'eye, like the ear, may think in octaves'. He felt that it might be possible to convert an octave of music directly into an octave of light. He bravely attempted to do this but was apparently unsuccessful.[4] The concept, though, is appealing.

One other musical term I'd like to mention is resonance. When two sources capable of vibration are at the same pitch, then as one vibrates the other does so as well, sympathetically. This phenomenon has physical as well as musical import as the people of Jericho found to their collective dismay.

Sound is composed of waves, pressure differences in the air, which cause our eardrums to vibrate and set up nerve impulses to our brains where our 'quiet' (*sic*) hemisphere presumably decides whether the sound is pleasant or not. In this sense of patterns in the air, sound has form. We have seen how sound can produce physical effects on matter by resonance. There is a formal system of study for such effects. It involves the study of wave forms and the way in which these forms influence matter. It is termed 'cymatics'.

In the eighteenth century Ernst Chladni observed that when sand was scattered over a plate attached to his violin the sand sifted itself into beautiful regular forms which transformed themselves according to the note played. 'Chladni's figures', as they are termed, demonstrated that the form was a function of pitch. Jenny studied these figures with more sophisticated methods and coined the term 'cymatics' to define this area of waves interacting with matter. His classic finding was that the spoken letter 'O' has a *shape* indistinguishable from the letter: i.e. the form of 'O' is the same as its sound.[8]

So sound has form in one sense or another and our senses feed this form into our brains where we interpret it. It is when we feed in the form of sound termed 'music' that the term 'interpret' seems inadequate somehow. D. V. Morano has described music thus:

> . . . Music is the language of our inner selves. In other words, music will be described as the language of human subjectivity. A specific piece of music need not arouse any specific emotion or sentiment such as sadness or joy, it simply gives us back to ourselves with all our idiosyncracies. Thus music is not a language in the sense of communicating specific ideas or emotions of the composer . . . Music is the composer's articulation of a pattern and beat and texture of sounds. Music is a language in as much as each one of us can be touched directly by a piece of music and given direct vision of our own subjectivity in a way of which no other human expression is capable. The rhythm of nature itself—of night and day, of the tide of the sea, of winter and summer—may evoke in us the same self-awareness as music, but we do not have the same mastery over the cycles of nature as we have over music, a product of man and therefore within his dominion.[10]

In the last sentence of this quotation Morano equates the rhythm of Nature with music. If indeed the two may 'evoke in us the same self-awareness' one might expect them to demonstrate common *form*. This idea, or course, is not new. It is thought to have originated on the island of Samos over two thousand years ago.

Around 580 B.C. Pythagoras was born on Samos. Although neither he nor his followers left any any written history of their work or beliefs, 'Pythagoras' thought' has been of very major import in the development of Western thought. Perhaps the fact that there *is* no written record of their beliefs has helped popularize some of the suspiciously apocryphal tales related concerning Pythagorean beliefs and practices.

Among the various discoveries credited to Pythagoras himself was that of the relationship between musical intervals and numbers. Like his fellow sages, Pythagoras knew that a single taut string when vibrated produced a basic or fundamental note. What apparently he alone discovered was the fact that only notes produced by dividing this string by *whole* numbers were in harmony with the fundamental. If the string wasn't divided by whole numbers the notes produced were discordant with the fundamental.

For example, the chord of C major is composed of the harmonious notes C (fundamental), E and G. If we stretched

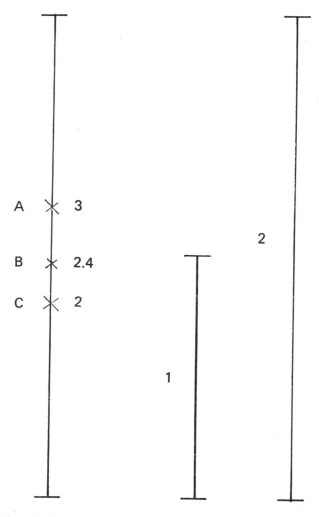

Points *A* and *C* when depressed will sound a note which is in harmony with the fundamental as they divide its length by a whole number. As Point *B* doesn't, the note produced by depressing the string here will be discordant.

A string twice the length of another will produce the same note when vibrated but it will be one octave higher.

Figure 20: Number and harmony

TABLE 4

Qualities attributed to numbers

---

1. Active
   Assertive

2. Passive
   Subordinate

3. Expressive
   Fortunate

4. Inexpressive
   Unfortunate

5. Versatile
   Uncertain

6. Simple
   Settled

7. Spiritual
   Hidden

8. Materialistic
   Overt

9. 'Highest' qualities
   mental and spiritual.

These qualities are representative of those used by modern numerologists who would imply that the Pythagoreans attributed similar qualitites to number. Note the polarity in the scheme.

out a string until it gave off the note C on vibration, then the notes E and G could only be produced by dividing (depressing) the string in a whole number ratio. (Fig. 20) It is also claimed that Pythagoras demonstrated the fact that when you double the length of a vibrating string the new note which sounds is the octave of the original one.

What Pythagoras had demonstrated, therefore, was that what we consider to be aesthetically pleasing sounds are correlated with whole numbers. Now this was a rather remarkable finding, and to the Pythagoreans it demonstrated that Nature and Man were in harmony and in some way numbers, whole numbers, symbolized this harmony.

It is not surprising that numbers were held in such awe by these people. These abstractions of the mind were waiting to be discovered 'outside' and the universe seemed to be structured in a form consistent with simple arithmetical relationships. Even today we can juggle with more sophisticated and even more abstract numbers and, in so doing, find that they are still out there waiting to be discovered in their interrelationships and power. When Einstein, *en passant,* scribbled $E = mc^2$, the universe was releasing to him the arithmetic of the atom bomb, the explosive music of matter-waves.

The Pythagoreans held numbers in such esteem that they attributed particular qualities to them (Table 4) and these qualities have formed the basis for the occult use of numbers in the art of numerology. Perhaps they related these qualities to music, finding esoteric significance in the sounds produced by vibrating strings divided by different 'qualities' of numbers. Perhaps not. What they did relate number, and hence music to, however, were the planets.

They believed that as the planets orbited the Earth they gave off music whose 'inaudible pitch' related to the velocity, and hence the orbital period, of the planet. Presumably they thought that this 'Harmony of the Spheres' resonated with Man and thus we were linked to the cycles of Nature. Such an idea of the wandering planets whispering out music and harmony is elegant and seems fanciful. In fact it is probably true.

As musical scales are related to numbers, the obvious way

to assess the concept of the harmony of the spheres is to look for numerical relationships between the planets. One of the most used, and perhaps abused, of such relationships is Bode's law, discovered by Titius but popularized by Bode in 1776. This relatively simple law states that the distance of the planets in Astronomical Units (distance from Earth to the Sun) follows a simple whole number relationship.[+]

Bode's law works well for most of the planets, Pluto being the major exception. It would appear that the law is the manifestation of the fact that strongly interacting bodies such as planets tend to settle in orbits whose periods are small integral fractions of one another. A number of systems of numerical juggling with the planets have been derived and contrived and these are well reviewed in Dean.[3] Some correlations with music emerge.

Johannes Kepler demonstrated that the ratios of the movements of the planets at the times they were closest to (perihelion) and furthest away (aphelion) from the Sun reduced to the ratios of a musical scale. This observation apparently kept alight his enthusiasm for planetary harmony in a musical sense.

In 1975 Schmidt indicated that the synodic periods[*] of the planets were closely in the ratio of simple whole numbers, and hence could be equated with musical intervals. For example, the ratio of the synodic period of Mars to Venus is 4/3: and the interval 4/3 is equivalent to a musical fourth. Similar relationships exist between other planets. Perhaps the most striking arithmetical manoeuvre in this context, however, was that carried out by Dean.[3]

He arbitrarily evaluated the 'planetary music' as follows. He took the period of rotation of the Earth round the Sun (year) and divided this by the period the planet took to do the same. He multiplied the answers obtained by the frequency of the note middle C and obtained surprising results.

[+]Distance = $0.4 + 0.3 \times 2^n$ where n = whole numbers.

[*] The periods which the planets take to occupy the same positions in the heavens relative to one another or to the Sun, Moon or Earth.

For the eight planets plus the Moon he obtained 5 Cs, 3 Gs
and 1 F all within a half-semitone of accuracy. (Figure 21)
Now, interesting as these relationships are, they may
simply demonstrate an underlying common, but unconnected,
mathematical relationship between planetary movements and
musical scales. The only way to know if the planets *do* play
music is to listen to them. At the gracious invitation of a
friend I did just this. I listened to the planets singing on tape
and I was impressed. The technique for imprinting planetary
sounds on to tape has been devised by an American, M. Heleus.
It is relatively sophisticated, and consequently the technically
interested reader is referred to the appropriate original articles
in the bibliography [5][6]. Enough here to say that by electronic means Heleus has converted planetary movements
into sound. The fundamental notes used in this work are

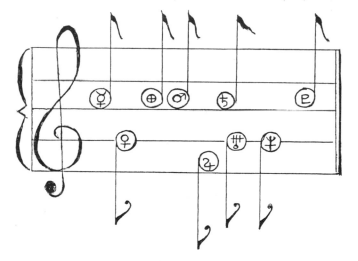

$$Frequency\ of\ planet = \frac{sidereal\ period\ of\ Earth}{sideral\ period\ of\ planet} \times frequency\ of\ Middle\ C$$

(Dean 1977)[3]

Figure 21: The planetary music
This figure represents the notes formed when the planets are
converted to 'sound'.

derived by scaling up the synodic frequency of two planets by 34 octaves to bring it into normal hearing range.

The technique is termed 'astrosonics' and the complexity of discussing it is increased for the general reader by the fact that it has been devised within an astrological framework. In general terms the concept is that each person's astrological horoscope (or 'chart') can be converted by electronic means into sounds which can then be played to them. Thus the planets and the relative angles they occupy with respect to one another in the chart can be directly experienced by the person whose chart has been turned into music.

Because this technique has been developed in the astrological context, it is only fair to discuss my experience with it in the same context. I should stress that because of this the discussion will be kept simple, and I shall simply give edited notes I made at the time of hearing the tapes and the more expanded notes I made later.

I listened to the tape in a relatively quiet room with a friend, well versed in astrology, who scoured my chart as the tones played out. I was not informed until the tape had ended which 'planets' the tones represented. In other words, I felt my sensations and made my initial notes while ignorant of the significance of the particular tone I was hearing. The tones varied considerably. Some were sustained monotones, others were jagged and staccato. One interesting observation I made was that in almost every instance I found my eyelids flickered in response to the tones. The degree varied considerably though, and I only made note of it when it almost disappeared with Saturn.

First the Sun.[+] I could feel an increased pulse pressure but attributed this either to my anticipating fireworks from the

---

[+]I have commented on my experiences in relation to my birth chart for the reasons mentioned above. It would be useful for the reader to refer to the Appendix if necessary to comprehend what is being said in relation to traditional astrology. Some of the comments I make here were supplied by my highly astrologically-informed friend who played the tape to me.

Notes on astrosonics tape. 17. 6.78, 16.30 B.S.T.

Planet	Experiences
Sun	Increased pulse rate. Expectancy? Sensation of a 'hole' but not marked.
Moon	Powerful sensation of something slow in water. Mud, sludge. Could almost see this. Wondered if tape (background noise) was 'dragging'.
Mercury	Felt sleepy. Tired *not* relaxed.
Venus	Eyes blinked rapidly. Sex. Sensation of opening—a mouth? Mentioned intensity of effect.
Mars	Nothing.
Jupiter	Must be Jupiter. Distinctive bass tone. Some physical tremor vibration.
Saturn	Tremor, vibration, muscle shaking 'shook me to bits'. Much less eyelid movement though.
Uranus	Definite tranquil effect—like meditation. Gradually developed into genital sensations and incipient sexual arousal.
Neptune	Saw-cutting sound. Almost unpleasant. Verged on irritation.
Pluto	Definite experience of small breath into large breath. Like inflating a tube with a small breath and getting a big one back. Not audible—visual. Breaths rhythmic and healthy but in phase. Felt basic integration with big breath.

---

tape or the simple fact that I was silent and listening to body and tape. The sense of a 'hole': the sensation the tone produced was more a 'point', a pin-prick in something. In astrology the Sun represents the focal point of consciousness, the ego. A pin-prick of Self in the collective? The Sun also rules the heart in astrology, perhaps also pulse pressure?

The Moon tone was quite distinct. I could almost 'see' mud and sludge, though the sensation was hardly visual. Eyes open or closed made no difference—there it was, a distinct, vivid impression, for no apparent reason, of mud. The Moon in astrology rules Cancer, a Water Sign, and on the day of this experiment it was in Scorpio, another Water Sign. At the time I was listening to the tape, the Moon was in opposition(180°) in Scorpio to the Moon in my birth chart. In my birth chart the Moon is in Taurus—an Earth Sign. At the time I heard the Moon, water and earth were well mixed. Apparently water and earth produce mud!

Mercury's music made me feel sleepy. This is the opposite of what one would expect from him. He is the planet of communication and activity It may be that because in my birth chart he is in opposition to Mars and in Pisces (Water) he took the opposite viewpoint. Perhaps I was just getting a little bored.

When Venus sounded my sleepy eyes opened fast and closed and opened again, flickering rapidly, and I sensed something else opening. Something like a mouth. This effect was intense. Venus in my chart is in the Sign of Aries the assertive. What was opening? Perhaps Aphrodite herself

In my opinion at least the Martian tones would not have stirred even the most manic of band marchers. Except for the few obligatory eye-flickers, Mars did nothing to me. When I was given the key to the tones, I smiled self-satisfiedly at my astrologer friend. Being very strong in my chart, Mars should have produced fireworks indeed when activated. My self-satisfaction was soon put into perspective when it was pointed out to me that, at the time of the experiment, Saturn transiting (i.e. in the sky at the time of the experiment) was in conjunction with Mars in my birth chart. In other words, Saturn was containing all my Martian energy and hence nothing emerged. Look at my comments when (unknown to me remember) Saturn was activated in music. Mars shook him and me to bits!

Jupiter I knew was Jupiter. The 'music' fitted the planet perfectly and it was the only tone which apparently did so.

Oddly enough the astrosonic Jupiter was to me very reminiscent of Jupiter in Holst's *Planets* suite. The Jupiter tones did produce some tremor in my body. I was informed that this was because I have a Uranus (galvanic) Jupiter opposition in my birth chart.

Uranus, the galvanic, unpredictable, planet indeed lived up to his reputation for unpredictability. Initially his tones made me feel quite relaxed, indeed deeply relaxed. Gradually, however, he stirred up drives quite opposed to relaxation and I was rather glad when these tones became silent. I was not particularly interested in the astrological whys and wherefores of this one, simply in how to obtain a long-playing cassette of Uranus in his less relaxed mood!

Neptune's tones were unpleasant and I can only imagine the poor old chap had got his trident stuck in a piece of wood somewhere under the sea. He made me feel as if someone's fingernail was *about* to scrape a blackboard. The astrological significance of this was not evident.

Not so with Pluto.

At the time I was listening to Pluto's tones he was in conjunction (by transit) with Neptune. In my birth chart both are in the air sign Libra. Pluto is also strong in my birth chart, being in the ascendant. He is also astrologically linked with the unconscious or the collective unconscious. Presumably, therefore, I was the small breath, he the large, and the fact that we got on quite well together, but were slightly out of phase, means that if I can get an extra bit of push and catch up with him I can integrate myself with big brother. The astrology fitted the experience and the experience was distinct, though not dramatic. And there lies the whole experience really.

None of these experiences was dramatic. I was not driven to bed by Mercury, rape by Uranus or the Casualty Department of the local hospital by Saturn. However, the tones produced effects and, in some cases (Moon, Saturn and Pluto in particular), these effects seemed to concur with astrological tradition quite significantly. I have been moved much more by Beethoven and Schubert than by Neptune or the Sun but, despite this, on reflection these things seem to work. Like the taste of an orange, it can only be described by direct experience. At the end of this session I was left with the distinct impression I had nibbled a bit of the Pythagorean orange, but only a pip.

I would like briefly to mention another recently published study of Planetary Harmony described by D. W. Hughes in the journal *Nature*.[7] Planetary music of a different type has been but on record by Professor Ruff and Professor Rodgers of Yale University. To describe how they did this I quote from the article:

> The first 'fixed point' of their realization is the mean frequency of the Earth, which they set at 800 Hz—very close to the g"(a musical expression for the g note about an octave and a half above middle c). The second fixed point is the orbital period of Pluto (248 yrs) which they musically set to be 20 min. 42 s. Ruff and Rodgers have updated Kepler by introducing Uranus, Nepture and Pluto. As these planets have such low frequencies they have been simulated by a series of rhythmic beats—Uranus around 10 to the second, and so on. The long-playing record covers the harmony of the spheres between 27 December 1571 (Kepler's birthday) and 1835.

In this instance too the planetary tones have been generated by means of a computer. The 'music', however, is apparently not as aesthetic as the idea behind its production, as the author says, '. . . this record put on near the end of a party would be guaranteed to clear the room in minutes flat'

We shall return to a variation on the theme of music of the heavens later. Before then I should like to pursue further some aspects of number and form.

We have seen how notes sound harmoniously together when their relative frequencies form whole number ratios such as 4:5:6; this arithmetic correlate with musical appreciation applies to visual appreciation too. In the book *The Golden Number* M. Borissavleitch describes how people given a choice between various four-sided shapes tend to prefer one in particular. This one, the Golden Mean, has its dimensions in the ratio of 1:1.618.

As with music and number we see an aesthetic connection through the Golden mean between form and number. Accepted in this case the particular numbers involved are not whole numbers; however, they, or rather it (the number 1.618), is related to whole numbers in a way which hints of an ancient knowledge of its significance.

In recent years it has become fashionable to seek significant numbers in many forms from the Great Pyramid of Cheops to the distance between ancient monuments spread across Europe. Much has been said in criticism of many of these speculations, though personally I feel it would not be unreasonable to accept that at least some are true. One particular example of geo-arithmetic is, in my opinion, particularly fascinating.

In his book on Chartres Cathedral[2], Louis Charpentier tells how, during a conversation, a traditional tale about three tables bearing the Holy Grail was mentioned to him. One table was round, one square and one rectangular, and all the tables carried the number of 21 or 2 and 1 as Charpentier interpreted it. In Chartres the Eastern part of the Cathedral set aside for the clergy, the chancel or choir, is rectangular and its length is twice its breadth exactly. Charpentier pointed out that the mean of the diagonal of such a rectangle and its width gives a very specific measurement, 1.618, the Golden Number we all apparently find so pleasing.

Charpentier believes Chartres to be an 'instrument of music', a form built on numerical as much as hallowed grounds in order to contain certain 'mystique'. Be that as it may, it certainly seems that form is highly important and has qualities peculiar to it, mystical or not, which relate to number.

One of the most provocative writers on strange subjects is Lyall Watson and he has been particularly instrumental in popularizing the idea of pyramids as forms with function. Watson postulated that it is possible that all shapes have their own qualities and that 'these forms we see around us are the combination of environmental frequencies'. He states that 'The basic principle of cymatics is that environmental pressures are brought to bear in wave patterns and that matter responds to these pressures by taking a form that depends on the frequency of the waves. There are a limited number of frequencies involved, and Nature tends to respond to these in predictable ways by repeating a number of functional forms.' By way of example he quotes tree creepers, heated air rising and DNA molecules having helical forms, and manta rays, mollusks and flatworms moving in exactly the same way. 'Given the same problem Nature will usually find the same solution.'[17]

Now this is a fascinating concept, speculative yes, but in the world of the quantum field it is intuitively sensible. Form defining function, form a manifestation of number.

In Nature we see ordered form all around us. Mathematically precise form, fitted to precise function. Yet no matter what environmental influences determine these forms, it is gratifying to note that there is still some touch of individuality. Take spiders' webs for example:

> Web building is inherited behavior; all members of a species have a specific design—a certain-sized mesh, for instance—but an individual spider's web is as distinctive as a fingerprint.[18]

Fingerprints of course come from fingers and most of us have ten of these, and thus most of us count from one to ten and then repeat ourselves. In fact, the Greeks stopped at four to reflect before going on to five as they apparently made the, to them, awesome discovery that the numbers 1 to 4 inclusive add up to 10. They enshrined this concept in the figure of the Tetractys (Fig. 22).

We have already mentioned the concept of form defining function and of form being defined by number through waves. Where does this line of thought take us when we're informed that 'some mathematicians . . . believe that numbers have an independent existence of their own and are merely observed by sufficiently intelligent mortals'? This concept is rationally 'unacceptable' until one adds up the facts about numbers. Then one wonders.

Numbers *do* seem to have strange patterns of behaviour, almost as if they indeed had an independent existence 'out

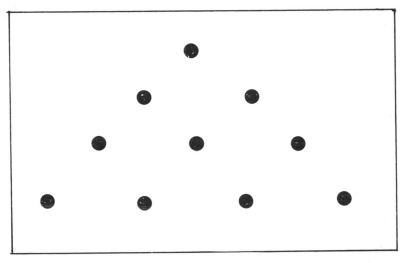

Figure 22: The Tetractys
This figure was considered to be highly significant to certain Greek scholars as it is structured on the numbers 1 - 4 which when summed add to 10 which being 1 + 0 reduces to the Prime Number again.

there'. There is no better example of this than the fact that probability theory works and the Law of Numbers, as we might term it, might well be considered to apply to the strange laws of chance.

In New York City, if a dog bites someone seriously enough the fact is reported to the Department of Health. The average incidence of reported bitings per day for the period 1955 1958 was as follows: 1955-75.3; 1956-73.6; 1957-73.2 and 1958-72.6! Despite the almost infinite variables which apply to dogs biting people severely enough to warrant an official report, the same number clocks up on average year after year. It's as if the Law of Number demands a biting total per annum! This particular example is quoted in Arthur Koestler's *The Roots of Coincidence.* In this book Koestler also quotes a case where a mathematician using limited data, almost *precisely* predicted the frequency of the number of soldiers kicked to death by their horses in a single army corps in a single year. As Koestler says, 'How do those German horses adjust the frequency of their lethal kicks to the requirements of the Poisson equation?'[9]

Numbers also demonstrate a biased autonomy. In an article in *Scientific American* entitled 'The peculiar distribution of first ·digits' R.A Raima demonstrated that, despite the fact that numbers in mathematical tables should occur with the same relative frequency, the number 1 accounted for 30 per cent and the number 9 for only 5 per cent![13] It would appear that this bias is real and follows some mysterious law.

Even at the most basic level, numbers show distinct properties encompassed in the fact that they are either prime (divisible by themselves alone or by one) or non-prime, i.e. composed of a set of primes (2184, for example, is composed of the set of primes 2 x 2 x 2 x 3 x 7 x 13). Thus even in this basic way numbers show 'form', the basic primes—about 100,000 of them in the first million numbers—giving rise to the rest.

Euclid demonstrated elegantly that the number of primes is infinite and Koestler (again) in *The Invisible Writing* describes what happened to him when he recovered this proof while in prison, scratching it on the wall of his cell with a piece of wire.

'The significance of this swept over me like a wave . . . leaving in its wake only a wordless essence, a fragrance of eternity . . . I must have stood there some minutes entranced, with a wordless awareness that this is perfect—perfect".'

Evidently Koestler had been deeply moved aesthetically by the power of numbers and this was no mean feat on behalf of our arithmetic friends as he was under sentence of death at this time.

Is it indeed too daring to suggest that number *is* 'out there' in the quantum field displaying its qualities through wave frequencies which give rise to form which, in turn, give rise to function? Probably! However, one of the most daring attempts to understand planetary periods in relation to us has been made through number, and the results suggest a link of number to wave and wave to form and form to function, albeit in a way as yet unexplained. This branch of study has been termed 'harmonics'.

We have already referred to some early harmonic studies in Chapter II where the fact was mentioned that polio victims were reportedly born more frequently every 3rd degree (or 1/120th harmonic) of the Sun's path round the Earth.

It was initial observations of this sort which gave rise to this exciting area of study which must soon interlink directly with cymatic and cosmobiological studies. A major pioneer in this work is J. M. Addey who has written a comprehensive book on the subject to which I would refer the interested reader.[1]

In effect, by empirical observation and application of standard mathematical techniques, Addey has evolved a scheme whereby the recurrence of mundane events in an ordered manner coincident with astronomical factors, is considered to be significant. The recurrence of the event creates a wave form which corresponds to a harmonic of a time fundamental, e.g. a year or a day. I will illustrate this concept by an example. (See Fig. 23).

The work of Michell Gauquelin is undoubtedly the best documented and the most precise in the grey area between causal and (apparently) non-causal cosmobiology. It has been referred to elsewhere in this book. Gauquelin found, for example, when eminent scientists and doctors were born, Saturn and Mars occupied certain positions in the heavens more frequently than should have occurred by chance expectation. In fact, Saturn and Mars tended to be either rising on the horizon directly overhead, setting below the horizon or directly underneath the new-born protégé much more so than should have been the case. For some as yet unknown reason, such babies are born when these planets occupy these positions.

Gauquelin leaves us with these intriguing but statistically significant observations, offering no explanation and letting them remain, as some authority who investigated them termed them, an 'absurd expression of an absurd experience'—whatever that means. Addey goes further.

As the earth rotates on its axis once approximately every

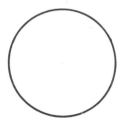

The fundamental can be any regular astronomical event. In this case we shall use the approximately 24-hour rotation of the Earth relative to the planets.

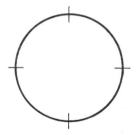

In this system, for findings such as Gauquelin's, the positions of the planets are considered to occupy harmonics of this fundamental period.

Hence Gauquelin's relation between planets and profession represents a fourth harmonic of this particular period.

Figure 23: Harmonics

twenty-four hours, then, relative to any place on Earth, Saturn will occupy any given position in the heavens once in that period. This period of rotation of twenty-four hours is termed, of course, the diurnal cycle. Addey would consider this cycle, of 360°, to be the fundamental wave of this system of correlation between Saturn and births of prospective scientists/doctors. (It could, of course, be the 360° of the solar cycle or the 360° of the lunar cycle, in which case the time of the cycle period would differ.)

He would then demonstrate that the recurrence of Saturn in the above-mentioned positions for these children constituted a wave-form which in this case he would term a fourth harmonic of the diurnal cycle fundamental. In other words, doctors and scientists are born when there is a pulse or beat in the wave-form constituted by the relative motion of the Earth and Saturn. This is astrology without the Signs of the Zodiac; it is music of the spheres beating in silent harmony. It is number, wave, form, manifestation, function.

This harmonic approach has been applied to many of Gauquelin's findings with much success, and planetary harmony seems to appear just about everywhere you look.

Gauquelin has shown a significant correlation between planetary positions in parents' birth charts relative to those of their children. Again Addey has found the harmonics, the waves, the numbers, linking parent to child. This observation is particularly interesting as at this level we can mix in biological circles (if not cycles), and we shall do this when we come to consider possible causes of these phenomena in the final chapter.

That, then, is a brief review of harmonics. You take your period of time—day, month, year or whatever—and call it your 'fundamental' (or first harmonic, as Addey does). Things rotate relative to it so you can express it as the 360° of a circle. You then sit back and watch events occur regularly in rhythm with your chosen fundamental. Be it children with polio being born every 120th harmonic (3°) of the Earth-Sun annual cycle, or scientists and doctors being born every fourth harmonic (90°) of the Earth-Saturn daily cycle, the factors are the same. Wave, rhythm, number, form. Earlier in this chapter I quoted D. V. Morano: 'The rhythm of nature . . . may evoke in us the same self-awareness as music, but we do not have the same mastery over . . . nature'. It is a poignant quotation in the world of astrosonics, harmonics and number.

There is a great deal more one could say on the topics covered in this chapter. Again we find ourselves confronted with things which seem absurd, but which evidently are not. Most of the things described have been scientifically validated, and none more so than the findings of Gauquelin which, for some reason, keep being swept under the scientific Establishment carpet. A few facts here and there may be unwittingly imprecise, but again it is the total picture that emerges which is significant.

I can think of nothing in science as fascinating and worthy of pursuit as the possibilities implicit in some of the facts and concepts we have looked at. While writing this chapter I have continuously had certain things slumbering beneath my conscious mind . . . the harsh facts of modern physical science in particular and, of course, the quantum field especially. I've wondered about mind and matter, whether number is a structure of mind or if mind is structured by number. So too matter. But such ideas are for others, better qualified, to pursue. What I wish to do is to offer some less exciting but perhaps plausible and, possibly, true causes of some of the interactions we have observed in this book between the Earth and our surroundings. I shall do this by looking at fields, electric current, lunatics and the pineal gland.

CHAPTER VI

'The Eye in the field'

In the journal *Medical Hypotheses* M. V. Viola described how superimposed on a steady increase in malignant melanoma were cycles of a markedly increased incidence of the disease. These cycles followed periods of maximum sunspot activity.[14]

Melanoma is a type of neoplastic disease or cancer which involves unnatural proliferation of the skin cells which contain melanin. This pigment, as we saw, gave rise to the term melatonin because in certain animals the melanin-containing cells are extremely sensitive to the effects of the pineal hormone. A melanoma, like any othe cancer, is a 'neoplasm' or new growth of cells which in the malignant state grow rapidly and infiltrate other tissues. In the benign state, while the rapid growth also occurs, the tumour cells do not infiltrate other tissues. Being much more parochial they remain quite distinct and are content to crush their neighbours, instead of moving in with them.

The cause of cancer cell formation, and the biological distinction between the malignant and benign cell types, is obviously a matter of much hypothesis and speculation.

127

Recently, however, a very eminent scientist, Albert Szent-Gyorgi, has put forward a particularly fascinating theory concerning the possible cause of cancer. He postulates that cells stop growing and replicating because of an inhibitory effect produced by *their own magnetic field.*[9] When the cell is damaged in some way, its field no longer controls growth and uncontrolled cellular proliferation occurs. Szent-Gyorgi's theory, simply outlined here, is in fact very sophisticated and he implicates a cellular substance, methylglyoxal, as being a major chemical in controlling cell growth. He contends that, by attaching itself to protein molecules, this substance enables them to conduct electricity and consequently produce a field. When this substance is destroyed too quickly in the cell, cancer results.

What is particularly fascinating about this theory is the concept of a field controlling growth, a cell-produced magnetic field, which should be sensitive to any influence normally affecting magnet fields. Such relations between cells, disease and electrical phenomena are not new, however.

R. Bentall,[1] in an article in *New Scientist,* reported on the value of pulsed electromagnetic fields in the treatment of conditions as varied as pain, bruising, inflammation and nerve regeneration. It is in the area of orthopaedics, however, that the science of electro-medicine has been most successful. One writer has described the findings of a group of workers in this area as follows:

> . . . While studying the natural repair of broken bones, C. T. Brighton et al. (Univ. Pennsylvania) learned that 'in the natural healing process, an electrical signal goes out from the broken area and directs cells to form new bone. Sometimes, however, perhaps because of poor alignment, excessive movement, infection or a host of other reasons, these electrical signals stop before the healing is complete.' They are now 'working with the concept of stimulating bone growth and repair by inducing carefully controlled amounts of electricity'.[16]

In the medical journal *Pulse,* Professor W. Sharrard reviewed this whole area of the use of electric currents to promote healing in bones. In particular he cited the work of Dr. Andrew

Basset et al of Columbia University who have had marked success in treating patients by electrical techniques.[12] In some cases these patients had bones so badly fractured that amputation had been scheduled. By application of electric currents to fracture sites, a cure was effected in 76% of some 285 patients treated.

In this same review the work of Dr. A. Pilla is also discussed. His group 'believe that in certain circumstances precise alterations in the cell's electrical environment can trigger specific changes in the cell's behaviour and that these changes can be brought about by time-varying electromagnetic fields originating outside the organism.' Professor Sharrard concludes his review as follow:

> It is clear from the very varied laboratory work going on throughout the world that if the correct signals can be found other cellular processes may be capable of amendment. The use (in orthopaedics) may be the first of many advances to be realized by diverse branches of surgery and medicine from the correct use of specific electromagnetic fields.

As might be anticipated, some physicians were highly sceptical of this work because of its innovative nature. However, the use of electrotherapy has recently come of age due to its recognition by the American Food and Drug Administration. This is the government-controlled watchdog on all medical treatments proposed or used in the U.S.A. It has now given its approval for the use of electrotherapy, hence silencing the sceptics. At a recent meeting on the subject held by specialists, the response was such that it was felt 'the proponents of the technique need no longer endure the scorn of colleagues'. According to Dr. C. T. Brighton, 'To put it bluntly, electricity works.'[8]

We have government approval therefore for stating that electrical currents and electromagnetic fields can alter cellular function. In the specific instances referred to these effects were beneficial: presumably under other circumstances they could be otherwise. If artifical devices can exert such effects, it is not unreasonable to contend that electromagnetic fields in the environment interact with those generated within cells and similarly affect cellular function and development. Indeed Dr. Frank Brown, who as we saw in Chapter II linked lunar and animal movements, has given us strong evidence for this, convincing evidence that changes in environmental fields can affect animal behaviour.[2] [3]

We have referred to the increased incidence of malignant melanoma associated with peak sunspot activity. During peak sunspot activity there is a tremendous upheaval in electromagnetic phenomena on Earth, as we have already discussed. Such changes will interact with living organisms and living cells. If the scheme proposed by Szent-Gyorgi is correct and the cell's growth *is* regulated by its own magnetic field, an association between sunspots and cancer is not difficult to propose. Let's not forget, also, that planetary movements correlate with sunspot activity and that according to Dr. Pilla '. . . if the correct signals can be found other cellular processes may be capable of amendment'. It is through this concept of fields affecting structure that we are led most intimately into possible explanations for the correlation between terrestrial and celestial events.

As should have emerged from our brief look at modern physics, the 'field' is not independent of matter, but a condition for its existence and a determinant of its form and function. This fact is true for us as much as for any other piece of matter. The 'field' referred to here of course is more abstract but no less real than the bioelectrical fields of cells. However the body is composed of cells and they produce fields which probably when unified correlate with the above attributes of the quantum field and resolve a question which has troubled physiologists for some time.

The problem of how the human body keeps its form, i.e. doesn't become an enormous cancer, has been one which has taxed many minds. There have been a number of non-physical factors postulated in an attempt to explain how, despite the dynamic physico-chemical processes which constitute our bodies, structural integrity persists. This 'force' has been termed variously 'entelechy' (vital force), 'embryonic field', 'organiser', 'biological energy', 'physiological gradient', 'biological field' and 'Gestalten'.

The most erudite and informative review of this topic was published in 1935 by H. S. Burr and F. S. C. Northrop, the former an anatomist, the latter a philosopher, both from Yale University. In their paper 'The electrodynamic theory of life' the authors discuss such problems of physiology in the context of the quantum field age. Their paper concludes:

> Furthermore, if the theory is established, it makes possible the application of the mathematical methods being developed for field and wave physics to biological material, thereby placing the study of biological organization on a mathematical as well as an experimental basis. (4)

The theory referred to was that:

> The pattern or organization of any biological system is established by a complex electrodynamic field which is in part determined by its atomic physico-chemical components and which in part determines the behaviour and orientation of those components.

This idea is very similar to Szent-Gyorgi's, though more general. Burr had the good fortune to discover the field he had himself postulated.

There are a number of accounts available of how Burr did this and of the various observations he made on this 'life field'. The interested reader is referred to these and I will give just a brief mention here of Burr's work. (5) (15)

Burr discovered the field by the unlikely method of rotating a salamander in a salt solution! He found that when he did this an electrical current was generated. As electrical currents are generated from rotating electrical fields, then the salamander was surrounded by one! So were other living things.

In fact every living thing studied exhibited an electrostatic 'life field' which ostensibly is produced by the chemical processes occurring in living organisms, and which in turn maintains their form. The potential difference of the field was found to vary with a number of factors, including race, sex, age and psychological state.

The field could be detected at a distance from the body, and Burr found that its electrical potential altered *in concert* with specific physiological events. The field potential changed at the exact time of ovulation (which he observed by microscope in rabbits) and at the time of menstruation in young women. It also changed its electrical potential over diseased areas of the body and, in fact, this potential change was apparently evident *prior* to clinical manifestation of the underlying desease. In other words, we are led in the direction of a field change *causing* or *correlating* with structural change and pathology, i.e. in the direction of Szent-Gyorgi and his cancer cells theory

Monitoring the electrostatic field in trees on a long term basis, it was reported that the electrical potential varied in strength according to certain periods. There was a daily cycle with a minimum at midnight and a maximum in the afternoon. There was an annual cycle with maxima and minima at the times of the equinoxes and a cycle in phase with the sunspot cycle. It was also reported that the Moon influenced the potential of the field, albeit relatively weakly. This last observation is reminiscent of the reported observation by Ravitz that the body field was altered in patients who were mentally ill, and that in some such patients the field change altered with lunar phase. Burr also reported significant field changes in schizophrenics.

So we find a reported correlation between 'life field', perhaps the most significant physiological concept of all, and celestial events. And so I feel at this point we can profitably attempt to synthesize the major points I've discussed in this book.

My intention is to demonstrate that there are a number of *possible* causal explanations for observed correlations between celestial events and events on Earth. More importantly, however, I should like to suggest a mechanism whereby celestial events at the time of birth, and in the early post-natal period, could *contribute* to the physical and psychological development of the individual in later life. It is useful to look hard at a particular case to describe a general one. Consequently I wish to relate my arguments mainly to possible celestial correlates of schizophrenia.

I must stress that I am not for one moment suggesting that schizophrenia or any other mental or physical state for that matter is a product of celestial influences. My thesis is simply that a credible case can be made for the involvement of celestial factors in our physical and mental development from birth onwards. I use the term schizophrenic as defined in Chapter I.

In Chapter I the fact that schizophrenics demonstrate a seasonal pattern of births was stated. There would appear to be no doubt that, whether in the northern or southern hemisphere, there is a significant increase in the births of schizophrenics in springtime.[13] Some studies have tended to vary slightly from this general rule. For example, one report in the *British Journal of Psychiatry* demonstrated a significant excess of *spring* births in neurotic patients, and *winter* births in schizophrenics [11] However, it would seem to be generally accepted that schizophrenics are born in winter and spring and not summer and autumn.

Seasons are a product of the movement of the Earth round the Sun, and children born in winter and spring are exposed to a specific photoperiod which is not evident in summer and autumn. The amount of light the child is exposed to will affect the level at which the pineal will function. The level at which the pineal functions may well, as we have seen in Chapter I, pre-programme certain glands in the body and pre-set the level at which they will function later in life. You recall for example how melatonin injections could inhibit onset of puberty in rodents if injected at a certain critical period after birth, and how subsequent maternal and sexual behaviour in animals could be altered by removing their pineals while they were young. Thus absence of the pineal, or excessive exposure to one of its major hormones in young animals, can influence future behaviour and developmental patterns.

In view of these facts a *possible* relationship between photoperiod at the time of birth, the pineal gland, and the subsequent development of schizophrenia (and other mood states) cannot be dismissed.

If the seasonal birth effect in schizophrenia is attributable to seasonal variation in photoperiod of the infant, then because of myriad variables in the child's exposue to light we would expect to observe an effect only when large groups were studied. This of course is what we find. Although the statistical significance of the effect is high, the absolute number of subjects who demonstrate it is relatively small.

So we have one astronomical factor, the Sun, which could, and probably does affect the general physiology, and pineal physiology in particular, of the new-born child. What others are there?

Living organisms such as ourselves are composed of a 'bucket of water and a bag of salts' and a fair amount of organic material. The salts, organic materials and water form uneasy mixtures of solutions and suspensions. In effect we are mainly constituted of organic and inorganic *colloids,* all dynamically functioning and inter-relating at a body temperature of around 37°C

In Chapter II correlations of astronomical events on colloidal systems were discussed, including the observations made by Piccardi that inorganic colloids underwent cyclic variations in physical properties with periods of one day, one year and eleven years. The eleven-year cycle was considered probably to correlate with the sunspot cycle, and the others to the daily and annual solar cycle. Note, however, the times of the sharp changes of effect found in the yearly cycle. March and September, Spring-time in the northern and southern hemispheres respectively. Peak times for schizophrenic births too. Piccardi attributed these March and September deviations to periodic exposure of the Earth to certain radiation belts during these particular months of the year due to its unique movement through the solar system.

We observed also the observations made by Takata on organic colloids, the altered flocculation index of blood correlating with sunrise, sunspots and with Sun-Moon eclipses. Again implicit in these observations is the idea of some celestial radiation significantly affecting biological systems when conditions allow it.

Observations pertaining to solar activity could possibly be accounted for by the radiation termed ELF (extra low frequency) waves. While these do not come to us direct from the Sun, they may arise as a result of solar activity. These waves fall within the frequency band of Burr's 'life field' and fluctuate at sunrise and at times of high solar activity and can also, apparently, affect living organisms. In particular they are claimed to be capable of affecting human reaction time, a good indication of neurological function. A number of suggestions have been made as to how these waves in particular could affect biological proccesses.[6]

The aqueous colloids of the body probably respond to these waves and other radiations because colloids are extremely sensitiive to such stimuli, and such phenomena can be very potent in making aqueous sytems unstable, especially if they are at a certain temperature, 37°C, body temperature. It is well established that water's chemical structure makes it beautifully unstable and ideal for living in.

Hence we have some definite biologically active 'radiations' such as light, heat, ELFs and some others, such as electromagnetism, which seem to be at least potentially capable of altering colloidal and hence biological function.

We mentioned how electric and magnetic field changes could alter biological systems and we have evidence that such changes significantly affect the behaviour of water, animals and people. All these radiations of course can be correlated with 'the heavens'. It was also mentioned in Chapter IV that the biological activity of metals 'must be sought in the stability, stereochemistry and magnetic susceptibility of their complexes'. This may be indicative of where we should be looking for links.

It seems then that a number of unobserved factors of celestial origin weave and spray themselves around us, affecting us subtly or less subtly as may be. At any given time all these various potentially biologically active radiations, and all the factors which affect them, can be considered as being one vast unified field of potential biologically expressive energy. Let's look at some of the factors we have considered which could constitute such a field.

A period of high sunspot activity sends sprays of radiation over us. Sunlight and heat stream down adding to the field. In September or March the Earth spins silently through a belt of Piccardi's radiation—another part of the field. If we are in Bavaria, or another susceptible place, the *foehn* may just be picking up and a spray of positive ions is scattering itself depressingly through the air. And these are just a few of the fragments which constitute our biological radiation field.

Now let's return to our particular case within the model being proposed for celestial influence and consider the entry into this life of a child destined to become 'schizophrenic' Firstly he is probably carrying a gene which predisposes him biochemically to the disease. He emerges from the womb and is exposed to a plethora of radiations, including those we have discussed as being potentially or actually biologically active. The development of his pineal gland and other physiological components will respond to the biological field surrounding him. This may conveniently be split into light, or photoperiod, and the other factors we have mentioned. Some if not all of these will be of an intensity contingent on the child's place and time of birth.

Light can affect pineal function in the ways we have described. by effects on receptor growth and/or on melatonin synthesis. The other bioactive radiations can potentially produce changes in colloidal structure and hence in subtle development of the gland. Thus, in the midst of this field of biological coercion, the pineal forms and moulds, is programmed and pre-programmes.* (Figs. 24 and 25)

As the child grows his programme unfolds and he becomes what his genes and genesis have made him. But this occurs

---

*We refer our discussion to the pineal here. The same principles would apply to other susceptible physiological units and sub-units, e.g. nerve cell connections, receptors etc. Neurological inter-connections particularly should be sensitive to such influences. The prime significance of the pineal in the context of this book is that it is probably the regulator of all body clocks, it has pre-set itself around the time of birth, and it can pre-programme behaviour.

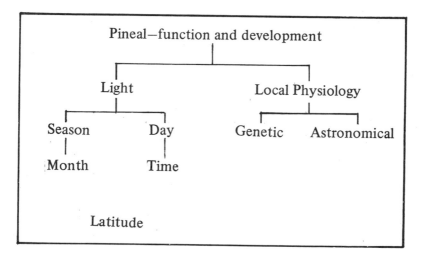

Figure 24

within the confines of his environment. The environment plays its part mentally and physically. He will be exposed to conflict, indecision, status awareness and the double-bind situations which tear him slowly apart. He will be exposed to accident, infection, nutritional vagaries, solar flares and storms of positive ions. In time these effects take their toll on the predisposed individual; he succumbs and the disease manifests itself.

Now despite the fact that, as I've stressed, this is simply a model situation to illustrate a more general point, it may still be considered too speculative. I don't believe it is.

Recently there has been much discussion in the medical literature concerning the possible role of the pineal in schizo-phrenia.[10] Not only is none of it inconsistent with what I've suggested above, but indeed my suggestions, suitably modified, could well explain some of the apparent problems experienced by those involved in this debate.

There *is* a definite link between season of birth and development of schizophrenia and hence between this disease and month and photoperiod at the time of birth. Photoperiod

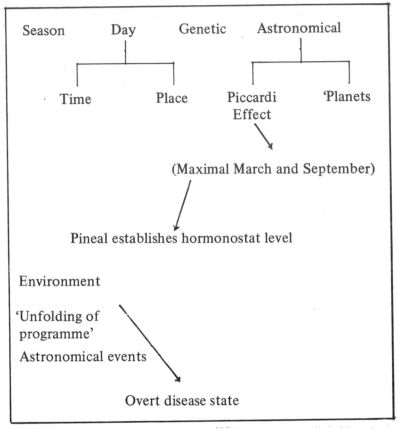

Figure 25: Possible preprogramming in schizophrenia

affects pineal function with special effects occurring in the neonate. Schizophrenia has been ameliorated by pineal extracts; pineal hormones have been claimed to produce hallucinations and other mood changes. Animals without pineals don't appear to respond to hallucinogenic drugs and there have been long historical associations between the pineal and mental health. Far from being too speculative, this model may even have something to contribute!

Obviously this model given for the schizophrenic could

also apply otherwise By similar mechanisms individuals could be predisposed to develop into other specific physiological and psychollogical types. This in turn could predispose them towards being specific personality types, and hence give some possible causal basis for the observations made by Eysenck et al., discussed in Chapter II, showing correlation between personality types and Signs of the Zodiac. It could also predispose them towards choice of specific professions and hence give a similar possible causal basis for some of Gauquelin's observations. It's not, of course, that simple.

One advantage of using 'schizophrenic births' as a model to examine celestial events in relation to our development is that they demonstrate a seasonal cycle which can be related to the movements of the Sun and thus to major effects on the pineal. The seasonal cycle, or at least its monthly division, also of course gives us a rough division into the Signs of the Zodiac.

Although Eysenck's initial results on personality type used the same basis, viz. division by astrological birth sign, subsequent positive studies on extroversion, introversion and celestial correlates *and* Gauquelin's studies on professions, showed correlations between these things and *planetary* positions, not the Signs of the Zodiac. So if we use the same model we lose our major regulator of the pineal—the Sun.

This suggests that, if our model is justified, in such cases planetary positions alone, relative to the newborn child, must account for differences in pineal function which will manifest later as distinct personality types.

This implies more subtle effects, but again let's not forget the all-important fact—when we achieve correlations such as those found between planetary position and choice of profession, the *absolute number* of people involved is small. Thus, although the correlation is statistically valid, it doesn't take many people in absolute terms to make it so. Hence a subtle effect can be identified if a sufficiently large sample of subjects is used, and only a few of them relatively deviate from chance. i.e. respond to the effect. So if there *is* a subtle planetary effect on the pineal, what is it?

It may well be simply an effect of planetary positions on local and cosmic radiation, on sunspot activity and the like, which, by altering biological activity in the pineal (and elsewhere too), would produce adequate physiological changes to account for the correlations observed.

A *direct* effect of the planets in this context is unlikely. Neither gravitational, electromagnetic nor other known effects are sufficiently large, compared with other astronomical factors, to impress themselves on us so apparently significantly. The planets do, however, spin around us relatively closely and it is highly speculative but possible that we could find a causal basis for their reported effects in a resonance phenomenon.

If planets set up resonance in the fields we have described which have potential biological expression, then these fields could resonate in turn with the body field and hence subtly affect physical, and so psychological, development. The frequency the planet generated would be expected to equate with the effects or correlates it produced.

Hence, for example, the frequency generated in the biological field by Mars might be expected to manifest itself in physical changes which lead to specific character traits. Those generated by Jupiter to others, and so on. While there is no direct evidence for such a phenomenon, it is scientifically credible; it could account for some of the results obtained by Gauquelin et al. and there is a some indirect evidence to imply its existence. For a fuller discussion of this refer to Dean 1977 [7]

The effects of the planets could, on the other hand, be more specific. We saw in Chapter IV how various planets ostensibly affected metal ion activity. If iron or other metals' metabolism were so affected by a specific planet, it could potentially alter pineal function as iron ions partially control the rate of pineal production of melatonin, and hence produce a specific predisposition of personality type with the attendant effects mentioned above. Such effects on any metals of course would potentially affect innumerable biochemical processes throughout the body. At present, however, such observations, in my opinion, remain unverified. If they *are* rigorously verified they will present us with problems of explanation which would probably require 'explanations' in acausal terms. As we say in Chapter III, however, Jung supplied us with a basis for such explanations.

One can argue, then, that cosmic influences affect us physically through effects on our developing and dynamic biological structure, and at the time of birth such effects may pre-programme us in a certain way, possibly via such effects on the pineal gland.

Our bodies, too, as we saw in the beginning of this chapter, respond to electromagnetic fields at the cellular level, and indeed seem to emit and co-exist with an 'organizing field' as described by Burr. So, in this context we can consider the possibility of the pre-programming of the individual from the time of birth by variations in the development of electrostatic fields in special key structures in the body, which would obviously include the pineal.

All the factors which can affect the bioelectric environment of the individual could potentially impress upon him their collective mark. The electrostatic milieu into which the child enters will affect things such as nerve cell connections, receptor growth on organs and glands and, in some cases, may significantly affect development of these physiological entities and others.

As an extension to this approach, if we assume that Burr's bioelectric field is indeed involved in a dialectic with the body, then we can postulate that the general electrical milieu exerts its effects through that. By causing an electrical change in one part of the field, for example, a correlated change in gross bodily function will occur. Again, this electrostatic environment will be, partly at least, contingent on the astronomical scene and on season and time of birth.

From this viewpoint our model schizophrenic becomes more a ball of electrostatic energy being pushed and pulled, like a charged amoebic ghost, by the electrical fields swirling and resonating, in the true sense of the word, in the wake of celestial events. Through time this pushing and pulling does enough damage for an imbalance to take place, so a short occurs, a fuse blows. Although this imbalance may materially manifest as increased receptor propagation in the pineal, or in the secretion of certain chemicals in the patient's urine, our conceptual framework has now taken a step back as it were from the gross physical world into one which is more shadowy

Here electric currents and electric fields weave and wave in Burr's 'biological mathematics' Progressively there is more unity, more merging, as things interact at ever more fundamental levels. If indeed the field and the living thing are mutually dependent entities, then a change in respective field potentials when I stroke a rabbit, for example, is a more unified statement of the event than the pleasant sensory picture it produces.

In this framework, where everything involved is considered to be composed of an organizing electrostatic field and a physical correlate, both of which are inter-dependent and manifestations of one another, the relation of celestial to mundane is more acceptable. Here the principles of harmonics and cymatics become obvious, the spinning planets setting resonating changes in the bioelectric fields, which manifest in turn in physical change and mood change. It is at this level that number and form and the arithmetic expression of form and function begin to whisper to us. It is here that the rhythmic harmony of the spheres plays in interweaving silence.

When we consider some of the areas we have investigated throughout this book, it is not difficult to find a place for a planetary involvement in this scheme: the planetary rhythm of astrosonics, the seemingly symbolic correlations between planetary movements and positions and physical phenomena such as heat and electrical conductance; the relation of planets to number, number to form, form to function. These and other equally tantalizing observations seem to hint at the true significance of the planets in the nature of things.

Equally the games and loaded dice of the post-Newtonian world, the acausality of the Jungians, and other mysterious phenomena make not too unreasonable the alchemical concept of Man as, in some way, a reflection of his cosmos.

We have gone from the chemical constituents of the body to the electrical field constituent as it were, in which case the pineal may be feeling a trifle neglected. There is no reason at all, however, to reduce its significance. In the electrostatic field view the pineal may well play a major role. I shall not speculate on this but simply remind you of its supposed role as the Crown Chakra, and the seat of the soul, the part of us which communes with that which in around us and produces a sensation of 'light' when stimulated.

Electrostatic field interactions are fascinating, and concepts and findings such as Burr's electrodynamic one equally so. However, our knowledge of the physical world has gone further than this, and at its limits are the marvels of post-Newtonian physics. It is here that we must attempt to consider things finally and so we are led to probably the most basic level at which we can contemplate the relationship between ourselves and our surroundings. In place of electrostatic fields interacting with one another, we become part of the quantum field. All of us and all of the universe as one co-existent inter-dependent field. Space-time, matter, mind, all mixed in the universal fabric. Our bodies are areas of field concentration like any other piece of physical matter, our thoughts perhaps areas of less intense concentration and more able to 'move' in space-time—to remember, reflect, dream.

There is no need, nor are we able, to explain cause and effect within this framework. It is all one, and what happens in the part we term the Sun reverberates in the Moon, the stars, in us and everywhere else.

Viewed from the possibility of this framework the correlations we have discussed between events on Earth and those in the heavens would be merely bugs on a sphere, intimations of other things. Thus, ultimately, our reflections on such events should carry us back through colloids and radiations, through bioelectric fields and resonating frequencies to something more fundamental. The quantum field, an holistic universe. The cosmos. Unification.

It is poetic to think that in such a system the concentration of 'field', the entity we term the pineal gland is the focus around which reverberate the lesser field concentrations of mind and thought. In other words, that it's much as Descartes said it was.

The Astrological Framework

In the period of time we term a year, the Earth moves round the Sun in an eliptical orbit. In so doing it produces our seasonal cycle. The planets too, from Mercury to Pluto, also complete cycles of solar orbit, though the period they take to do so vary greatly. Mercury, for example, orbits the Sun in eighty-eight days, Pluto in two hundred and forty-eight years. Prior to Copernicus it was commonly thought that the Earth was static and that the universe and its contents moved round us. This idea today is not—in view of the accepted relativity of motion—as unacceptable as it was during the last century or so; however, it did mean that our forefathers considered the Sun and the Moon to be planets also.

'Planet' of course means 'wanderer', a heavenly body which, unlike the fixed stars, restlessly wanders across the heavens. Until the 18th century there were seven 'wanderers': the Sun, the Moon, Mercury, Venus, Mars, Jupiter and Saturn. Thereafter three more were discovered—Uranus, Neptune and, in 1930, Pluto. So if we hold traditional views, as astrologers do, we now have ten 'planets' of which one, the Moon, is well within touching distance.

If we are unrepenting traditionalists and *do* maliciously consider the Earth to be the centre of things, we will find that these wanderers are not very inquisitive. Each one of them follows an orbital path round the Earth which is rather restricted. It's as if they're obeying a 'keep off the grass' sign because they all huddle together in a belt round the Earth with the Sun's path as a centre. This belt we call the Zodiac.

At the time of the spring (vernal) equinox, 21st March, the Sun's orbit crosses the projected equator of the Earth. If we take this point and from it divide the path the Sun will continue on into twelve segments of 30° each and we have **the twelve signs of the Zodiac. The first segment is Aries, the second Taurus and so on (Figure 26).**

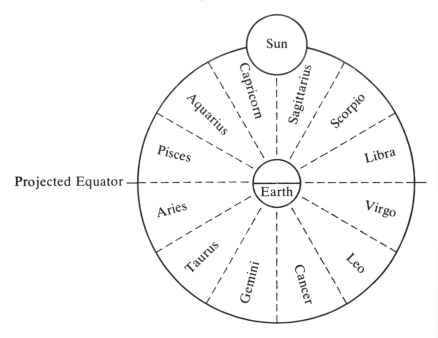

Figure 26: The Zodiac

If we now become *avant garde* for a moment, be astronomically chic and look at things as being *Sun*-centred, what this really means is that all the planets follow the same path as the Earth round the Sun and the width of this path is about 16° or 8° on either side of the Earth's path, which is termed the 'ecliptic'.

To return to the Earth-centred system however, it is now evident that the planets will occupy certain signs and degrees of the Zodiac at any given time. At a given time, for example, the Sun may be in 10° Taurus, the Moon in 5° Cancer and so on. It is eqully evident that, due to the fact that they move at different orbital speeds through the Zodiac, the planets will remain in different signs and degrees of signs for different periods of time. The Moon, for example moves round the Zodiac (i.e. orbits the Sun) once a month and so will spend just over two days in each of the twelve signs. The Sun spends about a month in each sign, and Pluto many years. Obviously when the planets occupy different signs and degrees of the Zodiac they will form angles to each other. These angles are called *aspects* and will be discussed below (Figure 29).

It must be stressed that the planets in the Zodiac are defined positionally only in two dimensions. If you imagine the Zodiac as a glass belt surrounding the Earth and divided into twelve coloured segments, then from the Earth you can look through the segments and see certain planets in certain positions in them. Although not evident to the observer, some planets are further away than others, however, so if two planets coincide by sign and degree, then although they will occupy exactly the same position in the Zodiac, e.g 20° Capricorn, they will not collide! An eclipse of the Sun by the Moon demonstrates the point well.

As well as making its annual journey round the Sun the Earth also make a daily journey round its axis. This twenty-four hour, or diurnal, cycle does of course produce day and night. It also produces other factors for astrologers to ponder on. One of these is the Ascendant, or Rising, Sign; the other is collectively known as the Houses.

If you imagine the Earth sitting in the centre of the belt

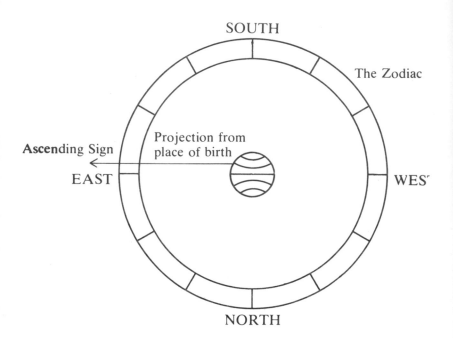

SOUTH

The Zodiac

Ascending Sign

Projection from
place of birth

EAST

WES'

NORTH

Figure 27: The ascendant

of the Zodiac, then during this twenty-four hour rotation the
Zodiac will revolve like a great wheel relative to the Earth. So
if you are domiciled at any point on the Earth during the
day/night cycle, the wheel of the Zodiac will revolve around
you from east to west with all its animals, people and objects
passing you with their silent cacophony. If, at the time of
your birth, you could project your finger out from the Latitude where you were born towards the eastern horizon and
touch the Zodiac, then the Sign and degree touched would
be your Ascendant sign (cf Figure 27).

If you take the Ascendant sign and degree as a starting
point and further divide this wheel into another twelve segments of 30° each, then you have the Houses. Thus we have
all the makings of a birth chart or horoscope.

A natal horoscope is a map of the heavens for the time of your birth. It shows which planets occupied which Signs and degrees of the Zodiac at that time and shows the angles existent between the planets (aspects). It also shows which Sign of the Zodiac was Ascending on the eastern horizon at your time of birth (Ascendant) and which 'Houses' (the twelve segments produced from dividing from the Ascedant) are occupied by which planets.

So this briefly is a sketch of what a horoscope is; but what is it used for, how is it used, and is there any validity in using it? Let me comment on each of these questions in turn.

What is it used for?

Astrology is used for many things, but fundamentally all its uses are contingent on the concept or doctrine of correspondences discussed in Chapter 4. In other words, the movements of the planets in the Zodiac, the angles they form to one another, their position at our time of birth, all reflect, symbolise and mimic what happens and will happen to us down here. Each Sign, House and Planet has a multitude of correspondences associated with it. and by knowing these and comparing the positions of the Planets at any given time with those they occupied at the time of birth, the astrologer can imply, suggest, or even predict apparently, what events are likely to occur in an individual's life.

But it is used for other things as well. Astrologers will tell you the most propitious time for making journeys, erecting buildings, or raising items on an agenda. They will tell you when countries will go to war, face economic collapse and (still) be subject to plague and pestilence. The milder ones, however, restrict themselves to deciphering psychological structure from the horoscope and do not, as some do, take into account your five prior incarnations (which are also hidden in the chart!) in their interpretation.

So respectable astrology mainly confines itself to personality assessment and trends. So how is this done using the horoscope?

In astrology the Planets are considered to represent energy principles, the Signs to represent modes of expression of these and the Houses to represent realms of expression. The aspects are considered to represent how two or more planetary energies will interact with one another. Let me attempt to illustrate these points by example.

The planet Mercury is considered to represent the principle of *communication*. The Sign Aries is considered to represent an *assertive* mode (as symbolised by the ram). The Seventh House is considered to represent the realm of *relationships*. If someone were born with a horoscope containing Mercury in Aries in the Seventh House, therefore, an (unsophisticated) astrologer would see the potential for fiery arguments (assertive communication) with spouses or friends (relationships). If Mars (principle: energy) was in trine (easy flow) aspect with Mercury in the chart, then the energy flowing easily into Mercury would—not to pursue a point too far—tend to make the arguments a little one-sided. Indeed, dialogue would probably become monologue! ('I know what you're going to say . . .')

In practice astrological interpretation should be much more sophisticated than this and a great number of factors are taken into consideration. This example and its interpretation, however, illustrate the process. Principles, Modes, Realms and aspect qualities are shown· in Table 5. Try for yourself to see how each planet would express itself by sign, House and aspect to other planets.

Now someone with Mercury in Aries in House Seven will obviously not always be bickering and squabbling with their spouses—even if they do have Martian energy egging them on! For example, someone who had this placing would find it difficult at one year old to do this, albeit they may well communicate energetically with their mother by ejecting screeching gurgles and ripping up their disposable nappies. No, the refined astrologer will tell you that the *potential* for this is there and that it becomes more likely, and may actually happen, when this potential is brought to the fore or set off by other factors. There are a number of these 'other factors' but we will consider only one of them: *transits*.

As we have said, the horoscope is the map of the planetary

Table 5
Examples of use of key word concepts in astrological interpretation

Planet	Symbol	Principle	House	Realm of Expression
Sun	☉	Self, The Ego	1	Self
Moon	☽	Response	2	Material things
Mercury	☿	Expression	3	Close family
Venus	♀	Harmony	4	Home or Base
Mars	♂	Energy	5	Creativity
Jupiter	♃	Growth: Development	6	Health
Saturn	♄	Learning. Awareness	7	Relationships
Uranus	♅	Change: Unpredictability	8	Finance. Emotions
Neptune	♆	Sense of ineffable	9	Travel
Pluto	♇	The Hidden: The Unconscious: Transformation	10	Career
			11	Social
			12	Unconscious

Sign	Symbol	Mode of Expression
Aries	♈	Assertive
Taurus	♉	Powerful: Steadfast
Gemini	♊	Communicative
Cancer	♋	Sympathetic
Leo	♌	Grandiloquent
Virgo	♍	Precise
Libra	♎	Balanced
Scorpio	♏	Passionate
Sagittarius	♐	Imaginative
Capricorn	♑	Reliable
Aquarius	♒	Independent
Pisces	♓	Sensitive

Someone whose birth chart contained the Moon in Aries in the Seventh House might be expected to *respond assertively* in matters concerning relationships. Such a person therefore might be continuously squabling with, or complaining vociferously about, their spouses.

Someone with Venus in Pisces in the Fifth House might be expected to seek to achieve a sense of *harmony* in a *sensitive* way through creativity. Thus they might be, or aspire to be, artistic in a fairly significant way.

---

positions at the time of birth, and the angles existing between the planets then we have termed aspects. Now obviously overhead right now the planets are still moving at different speeds through the Zodiac and forming angles with each other. The actual position of a planet in the Zodiac at a time after the birth time is called a transit, and the angle it forms in relation to the planetary positions in the birth chart is known as a transiting aspect. For example, if the Moon today is in 19° Scorpio it is said to be transiting Scorpio. If my birth chart has Mercury in 19° Scorpio then the Moon is making a transiting aspect (conjunction) to it. Obviously all planets make transiting aspects to the positions they occupied at the time of birth and some of these are of special significance in astrology. Saturn, for example, will return to the position it occupied at birth after about twenty-nine years and hence form a transiting conjunction (0°) with itself. This "Saturn return" is considered to symbolise a critical period in the life.

Astrologers thus would expect our example of Mercury in Aries in the Seventh House to be set off when Mercury was transited, say, by Mars. Then, they would suggest, the energies from the transiting Mars would set off the placement and they would suspect fireworks. In other words, the planets in the heavens would correspond to the events of man. Note that I did not say *cause*.

It is fashionable these days to consider the horoscope as *symbolising* the individual's potential, and hence the planetary movements and placements would correlate acausally with events on Earth. To this end many astrologers adhere to the Jungian concept of synchronicity which is discussed in Chapter III.

Is there any validity in astrology?

To answer this question we must define precisely what we mean by 'astrology' and, also, consider the end to which it is put to qualify for the term 'validity'. If we define astrology simply as an effect on 'the affairs of men' produced by the planets, then yes it is valid, as this book demonstrates. If one defines it in the accepted sense—that the birth chart and all the rest more or less determine what happens in a life, or whatever—then that's a different matter. An opinion on this is only formed after reading on the subject and also testing it* In his book *Mysteries* Colin Wilson says this of astrology:

> Astrology is the most pragmatic of the 'occult sciences' and from the scientific point of view the easiest to investigate. Any open-minded person who spends half an hour with a textbook of astrology will acknowledge that, for some strange reason, it acutally works. . .

Table 6
Use of aspects in astrological interpretation

Aspect	Symbol	Quality	Degrees of separation of Planets
Conjunction	☌	Neutral	0°
Sextile	✳	Easy	60°
Square	☐	Difficult	90°
Trine	△	Easy	120°
Opposition	☍	Difficult	180°

If Neptune were in conjunction with Mars in the Birth Chart, the person might have a vivid imagination or have particularly vivid dreams at certain times (e.g. when the aspect was transited, cf. text).

If Mercury were in trine with Venus the person might demonstrate exceptional eloquence, finding it easy to communicate harmoniously.

If Mars opposed the Moon the individual may respond to certain situations with difficulty despite feeling a strong urge to do so. Thus such an individual may respond to things aggressively even if this is unintentional.

---

*(A good well-argued book, putting forward the evidence for astrology is *The Case For Astrology* by J. Toonder and J. A. West now published in Penguin).

Bibliography

CHAPTER I

1. Altschule, M.D. (ed.) *Frontiers of Pineal Physiology*, MIT Press, Cambridge Mass., and London England, 1975.
2. Baum, M.J. *Science*, 1968, **162**, 586–87.
3. Baum, M.J. *Physiol. Behav.*, 1970, **5**, 325–29.
4. Cardinali, D.P. et al. *Proc. Natl. Acad. Sci. U.S.A.*, 1972, **69**, 2003–5.
5. Cook, N.Y. *J. Obstet. Gynecol.*, Editorial 1894. Cited in Altschule, op. cit., p 74.
6. Dement, N.C. in *Brain and Behaviour 1.* Mood, States and Minds ed. Pribran, K.H., Penguin Books U.K. 1969.
7. Dewan E.J. *Am. J. Obs. Gynecol.*, 1967, **98**, 656–59.
8. Elden, C.A. *Jap. J. Fertil. Steril.*, 1971, **16**, 48–50.
9. Eldred, S.H. et al. *New England Journal of Medicine*, 1961, **263**, 1330–35.
10. Fiske, V.M. *Endocrinology*, 1941, **29**, 187–96.
11. Ganong, W.F. et al. *Endocrinology*, 1963, **72**, 962–3.
12. Geller, I. *Science*, 1971, **173**, 456–8.
13. Hertz-Eshel, M. and Rahumunoff, R. *Life Sciences, 1965,* **4**, 1367–72.
14. Kappers, J.A. et al. *Prog. Brain Res.*, 1974, 149–74.
15. Kato, M. et al. *Proc. Jap. Acad.*, 1967, **43**, 220–23.
16. Kitay, J.I. and Altschule, M.D. *The Pineal Gland*, Harvard University Press, 1954.
17. Lerner, A.B. et al. *J. Biol. Chem.*, 1960, **235**, 1992–7.
18. Magendie cited in Altschule, M.D. op. cit. pl.
19. Menaker, W. and Menaker, A. *Am. J. Obs. Gynecol.*, 1959, **77**, 905–14.
20. Menaker, W. *Am. J. Obs. Gynecol.*, 1967, **98**, 1002–4.
21. Minneman, K, et al. cited in Altschule M.D., op. cit, p25.
22. Minneman, K.P. and Wartman, R.J. *Life Sciences,* 1975, **17**, 1189–1200.
23. Minneman, K.P. and Wartman, R.J. *Ann. Rev. Pharmacol. Toxicol.*, 1976, **16**, 33–51.
24. Mullen, P.E. and Silman, R.E. *Psychological Medicine*, 1977, **7**, 407–17.
25. Pavel, et al. *Brain Research Bulletin*, 1977, **2**, 251–4.
26. Sampson, P.H. 1972, unpublished manuscript cited in Altschule, M.D. op. cit., p209.

27. Timonen, S. and Carpen, E. *Ann. Chir. Gynaecol. Fenn.*, 1968, **57**, 135–8.
28. Torrey, E.F. et al. *Arch. Gen. Psychiatr.*, 1977, **34**, 1065–70.
29. Vaughan, G.M. 1970, 1971, Masters and Ph. D. dissertation thesis, University of Texas, Medical Branch at Galveston.
30. Winters, W.D. et al. *Neuropharmacol.*, 1973, **12**, 407.
31. Wodinsky, *Science*, 1971, **198**, 948–51.
32. Zweig, et al. *Proc. Natl. Acad. Sci.*, 1966, **56**, 515–20.

CHAPTER II
 1. Addey, J.M. *Astrol. J.*, 32/3, 1961.
 2. Addey, J.M. cited in West and Toonder, op. cit., p176.
 3. Allais, M. cited in Gauquelin op. cit. (18) p164.
 4. Bello, N.L. *This World*, 22.6.75, p22.
 5. Bondy, B. *Int. J. Clin. Pharmacol.*, 1976, **13/3**, 210–12.
 6. Bowen, E.G. *J. Geophys. Res.*, 1963, **68**, 1401 3.
 7. Bradley, D.A. et al. *Science*, 1962, **137**, 748–9.
 8. Brown, F.A. et al. *J. Exper. Zool.*, 1953, **123**, 29–60.
 9. Brown, F.A. *Am. J. Physiol.*, 1954, **178**, 510.
10. Chapman, S. *Scientific American*, 1956, **190**, 36–9.
11. Davis, W. M. and Webb, O. L. *Med. Exp.*, 1963, **9**, 263–7.
12. Cited in Dean, G. op. cit., p228.
13. Cited in Dean, G. op. cit. p499.
14. Dewey, E. R. *Cycles*, 1968, **19**, 232–8.
15. Fife, A. *Moon and Plant*, Society for Cancer Research, 1968.
16. Gauquelin, M. *L'Influence des Astres*, Denoel, Paris, 1955.
17. Gauquelin, M. *L'Heredite Planetaire*, Denoel, Paris, 1955.
18. Gauquelin, M. *Astrology and Science*, Granada, London, 1972.
19. Gauquelin, M. et al. *Br. J. Soc. Clin. Psychol.*, 1979, **18**, 71–5.
20. Hume, N. and Goldstein, G., *J. Clin. Psychol.*, 1977, **33**, 711–13.
21. Kollerstrom, N. and Drummond, M. *The Astrol. J.* (U.K.) 1977, **19**, 100–05.
22. Lieber, A. A. *The Lunar Effect*, Corgi, London, 1979.
23. Luce, G. G. *Body Time: the natural rhythms of the body*, Granada, London, 1977.
24. Mayo, J. et al. *J. Soc. Psychol.*, 1978, **105**, 229–236.
25. Mitchell, J. M. quoted in Cowan, R. C. *Christian Science Monitor*, 17.2.77., p6.
26. Nelson, J. H. R.C.A. Review March 1951, 26–34.
27. Piccardi, G. *Phénomènes astrophysiques et événements* terrestres, Conference at Palais de la couverture, Jan. 1959.
28. Poumailloux, M. *Bulletin de L'Academie de Medicine*, 1959.
29. Ravitz, L. J. *Am. Soc. Dentistry and Medicine*, 1970, **17**, 119–29.
30. Rensing, L. 'Biological Clocks,' *Rassenga*, 1971, **48/4**, 9–14.
31. Sullivan, W. *New York Times*, 23, 1, 76., p54.

32. *Sunday Times,* London, 4.4.76.
33. Takata, M. *Archiv. Met Geophys. Bioklimat,* **486**, 1951.
34. Tassa, J. et al. *J. Psychol.* **93**, p81–3, 1976.
35. Watson, L. *Gifts of Unknown Things*, Coronet Books, Hodder & Stoughton, London 1977, p162.
36. West, J. A. and Toonder, J. G. *The Case for Astrology*, Penguin Books, England, 1973.

CHAPTER III
1. de Broglie, L. cited in Capra, op. cit., p172.
2. Capra, F. *The Tao of Physics*, Bantam, U.S.A., 1977.
3. Dunne, J. W. *An Experiment with Time*, Faber & Faber, London, 1977.
4. Firsoff, V. A. *Life, Mind and Galaxies,* 1967 Edinburgh and London, pp105–6.
5. Firsoff, V. A. cited in Koestler, op. cit., p63.
6. Galvin, R. M. *Atlantic*, 1979, **243/2**, 53–61.
7. Glashow, S. L. *New York Times Magazine*, 18 July 1976, pp8–9, 27–37.
8. Gribbin, J. *Nature*, 21.8.75., pp619–20.
9. Hawking, S. W. *Scientific American*, 1977, **236**, 34–40.
10. Hoyle, F. et al. Letter in *Humanist*, 1975.
11. Jung, C. G. *Synchronicity: an acausal connecting principle*, Routledge & Kegan Paul, London, 1972.
12. Koestler, A. *The Roots of Coincidence*, Picador, London, 1974, p55.
13. Krippner, S. *J. Commun.*, 1975, **25**, 173–82.
14. Oppenheimer, J. R. *Science and the Human Understanding*, New York, 1966, p40.
15. Rosen, M. G. *Harper's*, 1978, **256**, 46–7.
16. Schmidt, H. *New Scientist*, 1970, **20/8**, 367.
17. Webster, I. W. *J. Am. Geriatr. Soc.*, 1976, **24**, 314–6.

CHAPTER IV
1. Burckhardt, T. *Alchemy,* Penguin Books U. S. A., 1974.
2. Dean, G. 'Recent Advances in Natal Astrology: a critical review 1900–1976, *Analogic*, London, 1977, p228.
3. Harvey, S. C. in Goodman, L. S. and Gilman, A. (eds.) *The Pharmacological Basis of Therapeutics*, 4th edition, Macmillan, London, 1971, p958.
4. Kollerstrom, N. and Drummond, M. *The Astrol. J.*, 1977, **19/3**, 100–105.
5. 'LSD for the Dying', *Sunday Times*, 31.8.75., p9.
6. Taylor, F. S. *The Alchemists*, Paladin, England, 1976.
7. Winters, W. D. et al. *Neuropharmacol.*, 1973, **12**, 407.

CHAPTER V
1. Addey, J. M. *Harmonics in Astrology*, Fowler & Co., U. K., 1976.
2. Charpentier, L. *The Mysteries of Chartres Cathedral*, Laffont, Paris, 1966.
3. Dean, G. op. cit., pp234–6.
4. Garner, W. *J. Soc. Dyers and Colorists*, 1975, **91**, 373–4.
5. Heleus, M. C. *The Astrol. J.*, 1975, **17/2**, 3–8.
6. Heleus, M. C. *idem*, 16–19.
7. Hughes, D. W. *Nature*, 1980, **283**, 607.
8. Jenny, H. *Cymatics*, Basilus Press, Basel, 1966.
9. Koestler, A. *The Roots of Coincidence*, Picador, London, 1974.
10. Morano, D. V. *Human Context*, 1975, **7**, 322–3.
11. Penfield, W. and Rasmussen, T. *The Cerebral Cortex of Man*, Macmillan, New York, 1950, p44.
12. Peretti, P. O. *J. Psychiatr.*, 1975, **89**, 183–7.
13. Raima, R. A. *Scientific American*, 1969, **221**, 109.
14. Ryan, P. *New Scientist*, 1976, **70**, 39.
15. Smith, S. M. *Hospital and Community Psychiatry*, 1975, **26**, 420–1.
16. Trotter, R. J. *Science News*, 1976, **109**, 218–23.
17. Watson, L. *Supernature*, Hodder & Stoughton, London, 1973.
18. West, S. *Science News*, 1979, **115/8**, 122–3.
19. Wilson, W. *Journal of Music Therapy*, 1976, **13** 39–48.

CHAPTER VI
1. Bentall, R. *New Scientist*, 22.4.76., 166–7.
2. Brown, F. A. et al. *Bio. Bull.*, 1960, **119**, 65–74.
3. Brown, F. A. et al. *Nature*, 1966, **211**, 830–3.
4. Burr, H. S. and Northrop, F. S. C. *Quart. Rev. Biol.*, 1935, **10**, 322–33.
5. Dean, G. (for example), 'Recent Advances in Natal Astrology: a critical review 1900–1976,' *Analogic*, London, 1977.
6. Dean, G. *idem*, p502 et seq.
7. Dean, G. *idem*, p508.
8. Editorial, *J. Am. Med. Assoc.*, 1980, **243/14**, 1401–3.
9. Holden, C. *Science*, 1979, **203/4380**, 522–4.
10. Horrobin, D. F. *Lancet*, 10.3.79., 529–31.
11. Parker, G. et al. *Brit. J. Psychiatr.*, 1976, **120**, 355–61.
12. Sharrard, W. *Pulse*, 2.6.79., 33–4.
13. Torrey, E. F. et al. *Arch. Gen. Psychiatr.*, 1977, **34**, 1065–70.
14. Viola, M.V. et al. *Medical Hypotheses*, 1979, **5/1**, 153–60.
15. Watson, L. (for example)*Supernature*, Hodder & Stoughton, London, 1973.
16. Weston, M. *Ebony*, July 1976, 54–61.

Index

* denotes illustration